DIFFERENCES
That Make a Difference

An Annotated Glossary of Distinctions
Important in Management

Russell L. Ackoff

Published in this first edition in 2010 by:
Triarchy Press
Station Offices
Axminster
Devon. EX13 5PF
United Kingdom

+44 (0)1297 631456
info@triarchypress.com
www.triarchypress.com

A catalogue record for this book is available from the British Library.

Cover design and artwork by Karen Ackoff.

ISBN: 978-1-908009-01-2

Contents

Contents

INTRODUCTION

In 2008, a year before his death, Russ had finished the first draft of his last book, *Differences that Make a Difference*. He called me one day and asked me to meet him at his apartment to discuss the book. As always, I accepted the call with a great sense of pride and enthusiasm, and went to meet him. He told me that he had collected many terms and concepts that he thought very important and, more specifically, that he thought would have tremendous implications for management if they were not clearly understood and the distinctions between them not made evident. Clarity and helping to explain terms and concepts were Russ's preoccupations in life. His seminal book, *On Purposeful Systems*, co-authored with Fred Emery, is a testimony to this fact.

Russ asked me to assist him with the necessary literature search to make sure he hadn't omitted any significant term or concept. I did the work and came back to him with a short list of some of the things I thought he should consider. Among them was "abductive logic", so-called by Charles Sanders Peirce.[1] I suggested that he should add Peirce's articulation of abductive reasoning to the section on "Induction versus Deduction". I told him that the literature on Design Thinking invariably discusses the importance of this kind of reasoning. For some reason (that he never explained to me), he wouldn't consider the term to be significant in comparison to inductive and deductive reasoning.

---

1   For an explanation of Charles Sanders Peirce's abductive logic, see:
    http://en.wikipedia.org/wiki/Charles_Sanders_Peirce

Even today, I remain curious as to why he didn't take this into consideration, especially as Russ studied philosophy for his PhD and later pioneered the application of Design Thinking principles in planning. More recently I was told that he was going to meet with Roger Martin, one of the proponents of Design Thinking and an advocate of abductive logic. Unfortunately, that meeting never took place.

Russ also asked me to help him with the publication of the book. This request coincided with a visit from professor Roy Marcus, the chairman of the Da Vinci Institute in Johannesburg, South Africa. At the time we were working with the institute to establish the Ackoff Center for Systems and Design Thinking in South Africa (a project that is still ongoing). Professor Marcus suggested that the Center should take a lead in publishing an expanded version of the book, containing some examples relevant to South Africa, and dedicated to the legacy of Nelson Mandela. Russ had a tremendous respect for President Mandela and he always considered him a systems thinker and a transformative leader. Sadly, Russ died before the project could take off in South Africa.

Since Russ was always very strict about the editorial changes to his writings, it was decided that the manuscript should be offered to a publisher who would agree to publish the book without any additions or changes to the original writing. Fortunately, Triarchy Press (UK-based publishers who had already published Ackoff's f-Laws books) offered to publish his two last manuscripts, including this one, without changing the original script. In discussing *Differences That Make a Difference* with the editorial team at Triarchy, I suggested we approach Charles Handy with a request to write the Foreword. Russ had the highest respect for Charles Handy and his writings. Specifically, he loved the fact that the two of them had independently developed the concept of a corporation as a community. From the year 2000 until the time he couldn't work any more, Russ had been instrumental in creating a community of practice that comprised practitioners who shared an office and its equipment and who, despite remaining totally independent, collaborated together around projects. That Charles agreed to write the foreword would have made Russ very happy. Additionally, I suggested that we approach Karen Ackoff (his daughter) to design the cover. (Karen had done all the illustrations for Ackoff's *The Art of Problem Solving*, published in 1978 by Wiley). You can see what a great job she did with her design.

Finally, although it makes me very sad that this work is the final book by Ackoff, I am also optimistic. Most of us who were Russ's students honestly believe that his professional reputation in management sciences will follow van Gogh's in painting—that Ackoff is yet to be discovered but soon to be revered by many.

John Pourdehnad ~ Philadelphia, USA ~ November 2010

Foreword

Russell Ackoff, who died last year at the age of ninety, was a scholar of international renown, a sought-after consultant to business and government, a wise observer of human nature and a very nice man. He was an early proponent of what came to be called Systems Theory or what he preferred to call the theory of purposeful systems. At one level this appears to be common sense, the fact that everything in a human system is connected, but, in practice, it means that you have to understand the whole in order to understand the parts, that reductionism, or reducing everything to its component parts, is dangerous, and that you cannot always, or even often, attribute specific causes to particular effects. You don't, Russell said, advocate brain surgery as the remedy for a headache. Instead you put a pill in the stomach. Nor do you put a Rolls Royce engine in a Susuki car to make it go faster.

It was that kind of homespun example that first attracted me to Russell. He was so confident in his scholarship that he could allow himself to use the vernacular and the commonplace to explain his ideas. In later life he gave full voice to his urge to explain the practical consequences of his long years of research. The first result was the book of f-Laws, also published by Triarchy Press, a collection of distilled and witty observations of bad leadership practices and misplaced wisdom that were too often paraded as so-called good management. Now comes this small volume of contradictions and differences.

In it Russell tackles, briefly and concisely, the confusions that bedevil much of our lives and lead to much mismanagement in organizations as well as in our personal doings.

Some of them are obvious, but all the more important because they are so familiar and therefore easily overlooked. Needs versus Desires, for example. Mistaking or misdefining a desire as a need has led many an addict astray and misdirected too many advertising campaigns.

The differences come, like Heinz, in 57 varieties. Russell lists them alphabetically, implying perhaps that they are all of equal importance. Personally I would single out two for particular attention: ANALYSIS VERSUS SYNTHESIS (pages 7-10), and ERRORS OF COMMISSION VERSUS ERRORS OF OMISSION (pages 45-46). Analysis without Synthesis leads to reductionism and the danger of mistaking the parts for the whole. An easy trap to fall into, but one that leads to paralysis rather than action unless followed by a synthesis. Equally important in life are the two types of errors. The things that should not have been done are easily recognized and measured. It is those things that were not done that could have been, and maybe should have been, that go unnoticed, and with them, too often, the creativity that would have led the way to the future.

As the title of the book puts it, these are all differences that make a difference. It is a manual for clear thinking, a fitting tribute to a man whose life was devoted to helping others to think both more systematically, in the proper use of that word, and more usefully.

Charles Handy ~ Norfolk, UK ~ October 2010

PREFACE

Browsing through a dictionary or thesaurus makes it clear that many terms and the concepts they represent have multiple meanings. Therefore, different terms often have overlapping meaning and hence are considered to be synonyms—for example, ethics and morality, and conflict and competition. Unfortunately, this frequently obscures or conceals important distinctions. A distinction is important if it affects the way we think and, more importantly, the way we act.

These differences may not be reflected in how we act in everyday circumstances, but they do matter when making decisions about policies and programs, both public and private.

Many disagreements and conflicts derive from the attribution of different meanings to terms or concepts. For example, is *competition* a good or a bad thing? The answer, as I will try to show, depends on the meaning given to it. The debate about abortion revolves around the meaning of *life*, particularly when it begins. How can we resolve disagreements and conflicts that derive from such ambiguity? This can be done only by removing the ambiguity. Hopefully, this is what this book does.

Russ Ackoff

Absolution versus Resolution versus Solution versus Dissolution

To absolve oneself of responsibility for handling a problem is to ignore it—let it alone with the expectation that it will either solve itself, pass away, or be solved by someone else. A manager who absolves himself from responsibility for problems manages by default.

To resolve a problem is to treat it in a way that is derived from past experience. This is done in one of two ways. In the first, a similar problem to the current one is recalled, as is the way it was treated. That treatment, with modification if needed, is then applied in the current situation. This application is directed at doing well enough, not necessarily at doing as well as possible. The second way to use past experience is to identify the source of the current problem and remove it from the position in which it can create the problem. That is, the source of the problem is identified and removed. This procedure is also directed at doing well enough— at satisficing. To satisfice is to satisfy and suffice, a combination that the Nobel winning economist, Herbert Simon, identified as the principal objective pursued by management when faced with a problem.

To solve a problem is to apply scientific methods to the problem— seeking an optimal solution to the problem, one that is directed at doing as well as possible in its current context. This way of attacking problems is characteristic of Operations Research and the Management Sciences in general. The techniques developed in these fields became widely used to solve problems, for example, linear programming, dynamic programming, inventory theory, and game theory.

Problem solving in this sense was developed to a large extent during World War II in the military. It first appeared in Great Britain but was quickly imported by the United States. This method, often called "quantitative analysis", was widely disseminated after the war but failed to be adapted to the changing context in which management had to operate. Once treated as a panacea for many of the problems managers faced, it is now restricted to a relatively small set of problems that lend themselves to scientific treatment, mostly production and distribution oriented problems.

Unfortunately, problems do not stay solved because either the entity that has the problem, or its environment, changes in such a way as to make what was previously a solution no longer effective. For example, one can dress for rain appropriately. If while out in the rain it stops raining and the sun comes out and the temperature rises into the 90s, the clothes that were effective in keeping dry in the rain are not effective in keeping cool in a dry hot environment.

Finally, to dissolve a problem is to redesign the entity that has the problem or its environment in such a way as eliminates the problem so that it cannot arise again despite changes in either the environment or the entity that has the problem. For example, in using the original paper book of matches distributed with tobacco products, matches were struck on an abrasive strip located at the bottom of the book. Occasionally a spark would fly off a match struck without closing the cover and it would hit one of the exposed matches. The pack would then explode and burn the hand that held it. When the manufacturers printed at the bottom of the pack, "Close cover before striking", it did not solve the problem. The warning was ignored by many users. The problem was dissolved by moving the abrasive strip to the back of the package. Now flying sparks could not reach exposed matches facing the front. This change of design dissolved the problem and its effectiveness was independent of changes in the environment.

Administration versus Management versus Leadership

It is useful to keep these three forms of guiding or directing others separate. Administrators direct others in the pursuit of ends by the use of means selected by a third party. For example, one who supervises a group of payroll or accounts-receivable clerks is an administrator. Others determine the output required of those s/he supervises and the means by which they produce it. Therefore, an administrator carries out the will of others through still others.

Managers are ones who direct others in the pursuit of ends by the use of means that they select. Unfortunately some called managers are really administrators, carrying out the will of others. It is apparent that much greater skill, knowledge, and understanding are required of managers than of administrators.

Executives are managers who manage managers. The chief executive officer and senior vice presidents of organizations are executives. Note: all executives are managers or leaders, but the converse is not true.

Leaders are ones who direct others in the pursuit of ends by the use of means that they and their followers jointly select. The followers of leaders follow voluntarily. Alleged leaders whose followers do so through coercion are commanders, not leaders.

A guide is one who shows others how to reach a destination they have chosen. Since a guide does not choose or participate in the choice of destinations, s/he is not a leader.

A coach is one who improves the performance of designated others in an activity they chose to engage in. Administrators, managers and leaders all may coach others in their performance— the pursuit of ends they, the others, select (see also GUIDE VERSUS COACH, page 58).

The two essential functions of a leader are (1) to formulate and articulate a vision of something that may or may not be attainable (an ideal) but toward which progress is possible without limit. (2) The leader must formulate a strategy for pursuing the vision, one that offers hope of progress toward realization of the vision. Another may have developed the vision articulated. For example, Marx had first developed the vision that Lenin articulated.

Leaders must be capable of inspiring their followers, that is, of making them willing to make short-run sacrifices in order to make longer-run progress. The ability to inspire others is an art, not a science. It requires talent that cannot be transmitted from one person to another.

Therefore, leaders cannot be made but those with the talent can be made more effective through education; talent can be enhanced. Almost anyone can be taught to draw, but none can be taught to be an artist. The works of artists can be improved, however, by their learning how better to use available and relevant materials and tools and techniques.

The vision formulated by a leader need not be a "good" one; for example, the ones formulated by Hitler and Mussolini. Leaders can lead evil causes.

Few presidents of the United States can be called leaders.

Washington, Jefferson, Lincoln and Franklin Roosevelt, perhaps, qualify, and among others Martin Luther King clearly does.

Administrator, Manager, Leader

Analysis versus Synthesis

Analysis is a way of thinking about objects and events that yields knowledge of the whole and understanding of its parts. It involves three steps:

1. Take apart the object or event under study.

2. Determine what each part does and what role it plays in the behavior or properties of the whole.

   This produces knowledge of what each part does and reveals its role or function in the whole and, therefore, understanding of the parts.

3. Aggregate the knowledge of the parts (how they act and interact) into knowledge of how the whole works.

This process yields knowledge of how the whole works but does not explain why the whole works the way it does. It does explain why each part works the way it does. For example, analysis of an automobile can reveal how it works (knowledge) but not why it works the way it does or is used the way it is. For example, it does not explain why the British drive on the left and Americans on the right, or why the motor is usually (but not necessarily) in the front of the automobile. However, if a car breaks down, analysis can reveal which part or parts have ceased working the way they should and, therefore, require repair or replacement. This explains the breakdown and so yields understanding of it.

It takes synthetic thinking to explain the behavior and structure of an entity as a whole or the ways it is used. Like analytic thinking, synthetic thinking also involves three steps, each the opposite of the corresponding step in analysis.

1. Identify a larger whole that contains the thing to be explained (i.e. identify the containing whole of which the thing to be explained is a part).

2. Identify the function of the larger containing whole.

3. Disaggregate the function of the containing whole to identify the role or function of that which is to be explained.

Analysis yields knowledge of wholes; synthesis yields understanding of them.

Scientific research is predominantly analytic and operates on the principle that the properties and behavior of an entity cannot be completely understood until its ultimate (indivisible) parts—elements—are understood. This doctrine, called reductionism, is responsible for the crusade that each and every branch of science conducts in search of its relevant elements. Physics once took this to be the atom, now partons and quarks; chemistry, the elements in the periodic table such as oxygen, hydrogen, nitrogen, etc.; biology, the cell; and so on.

Most of the organizations and institutions in our society are constructed and managed analytically. This is apparent, for example, in how a college's business school teaches management. It divides the activities of a business into functional parts: production, distribution, marketing, finance and so on, and teaches each separately as though each existed independently of all the others. The student is left to aggregate the alleged knowledge and understanding thus gained into knowledge of the whole. However, without dealing with the interactions of these parts the knowledge of the whole is incomplete. To understand the role of a part in the whole requires knowing how the parts interact as well as how they act.

If students are lucky, subsequent employment will provide an opportunity to gain such systemic knowledge.

Scientific research is the epitome of analysis; design is the epitome of synthesis. It is by designing something that we learn how it works as a whole—how its parts interact to produce the behavior and properties of the whole. It also raises to consciousness its functions in its containing systems. Analysis tells how the whole works. If an automobile stops operating, we need to identify the part or parts that have stopped working properly. This is required to fix it.

To understand why a system works as it does requires synthetic thinking: identifying the role or function of the whole in the larger system of which it is a part. Thus, the automobile is understood by what role it plays (its function) in the transportation system, not by how it does it. For example, an automobile is defined as an instrument that carries people and goods from one place to another under a person's control, in privacy and on land. Similarly, a computer is defined by what functions it can perform, not by how it does it.

This is why a person can drive an automobile or use a computer without knowing how it works.

If we think of systems as being of two types: natural, like trees, insects, and people, and those made by man, artifacts such as houses, automobiles, governments and societies, it becomes clear that design applies only to artifacts—things made by man. This is a major distinction between the natural sciences and those that deal with the products of man.

Capitalism versus Socialism versus Communism

Capitalism, socialism and communism are three different economic structures or states. They seldom exist in their pure forms although many states come quite close to it.

Capitalism is a state in which both the means of production are owned, and many of the services are provided, by non-governmental organizations or individuals.

Socialism is a state in which many if not most services are provided by the state but the means of production are owned privately.

Communism is a state in which the means of production and the providers of services are owned by the state.

In almost all three forms of government the appropriate roles of state and private sources remain ambiguous and are the source of many internal conflicts. For example, in the United States health care is subject to much argument as to its proper source. In some socialist states they argue about the proper location of banks and transportation. In some communist states small production units, usually a family, are privately owned and operated.

Cause-Effect versus Producer-Product

One thing is said to be the cause of another—its effect—in a specified environment if it is both necessary and sufficient for that effect. The effect would not have occurred if the cause had not been present, but if the cause does occur the effect must occur, again, in a specified environment. For example, my striking a bell in the room in which I am working (the cause) produces its ringing (the effect). This ringing would not occur if I did not strike the bell and would certainly occur if I did.

Note, however, if the bell were struck in a vacuum, it would not ring. This is why the cause-effect relationship is always relative to a particular environment or environments.

A producer is necessary but not sufficient for its product in a specified environment. If I plant a seed (producer) in my garden, it may or may not produce a flower (product). It depends on whether it gets enough water and sunshine, which are co-producers of the flower. Since producers are never sufficient for their products, there must be co-producers that are also necessary. A producer plus all its co-producers constitute the cause of the effect because they are sufficient for it as well as necessary.

Thus the essential parts of a system are producers of the system's properties or behavior, not their cause, because the product (the behavior or properties of the system) always depends on more than one essential part.

In ordinary living we deal more with producer-product relationships than cause-effect because at least some of the producers in any given situation of a desired product are not subject to our control. Therefore, if a producer occurs there is a probability its product will occur. But if a cause occurs, its effect will certainly follow. For this reason producer-product has also been called probabilistic causality.

Conflict versus Cooperation versus Competition

When one party's pursuit of its objective reduces the chance of a second party obtaining its objective, the first party is in conflict with the second. For example, if demonstrators prevent someone from entering a building they want to enter, the demonstrators are in conflict with the person who wants to enter the building. Anyone who prevents another from doing whatever s/he wants is in conflict with that other. Parents are often in conflict with their children.

If one party's pursuit of its objective increases the chances of the second party's obtaining its objective, the first party is cooperating with the second. For example, if a pedestrian helps a blind pedestrian cross heavily traveled streets safely, the sighted pedestrian is cooperating with the blind person. Anyone who enables another to do what s/he wants is in cooperation with that other. Parents are often cooperating with their children.

The so-called "zero-sum game" in which one party's gain is another party's loss is an instance of conflict. When one party makes considerable noise in an environment in which I am trying to think, and thereby prevents me from doing so, that party is in conflict with me. If a third party enters the environment and quiets the second party, then that third party is cooperating with me.

The meanings of conflict and cooperation are fairly simple and clear, but not so for competition. Consider a tennis match between two parties. Both want to win but only one can. They are in conflict over winning. But they are playing for recreation also, to have fun. They cooperate with respect to this objective, and it is the more important one. Therefore, the conflict serves the purposes of the parties involved in an aspect of competition. Curiously, the more intense the conflict with respect to winning, the more cooperative the parties are with respect to their common objective: recreation. It is no fun playing against someone who has no chance of winning.

Competition has often been defined as "conflict according to rules". There are always implicit or explicit rules in competition to assure that the conflict serves the cooperative aspect of the interaction. The objective being served by the conflict in competition may be that of the "players" (intrinsic) or of a third party (extrinsic). Thus, for example, the presence of conflicting sides in a professional football or baseball game serves the entertainment objective of the audience and the more intense the conflict, the more entertaining it is and the more pleasurable it is for the players. Therefore, competition can be both intrinsic and extrinsic simultaneously.

Rules alone do not convert conflict to competition. They are necessary but not sufficient. To be competitive the conflict must serve a common purpose in a positive way. War between two nations fought without rules (like those formulated by the

Geneva Convention) is pure conflict. If rules protect civilian populations but they still suffer as they do in most wars, the war is still an example of conflict. Even if the war is fought over the acquisition of territory, it is still conflict. The "purist" form of conflict is involved in war with terrorists who acknowledge no laws whatsoever.

A fight that takes place in a ring with rules governing the behavior of the opponents is competition. The rules are designed to assure the entertainment value of the fight. But in a street brawl there may be no such rules. It is "pure" conflict. However, if there is an audience and the conflict serves them, it is competition relative to the audience although pure conflict for the fighters.

With respect to conflict and cooperation there are three possible types of relationship between the parties involved:

1.   Each may be in conflict with the other.

2.   Each may be in cooperation with the other.

3.   One may be in conflict with the other while the other is in cooperation with the first.

Where each of two parties is in conflict with the other (1 above), the one who is affected least can be said to be a malevolent exploiter of the other. For example, in a destructive war, the one who wins is the malevolent exploiter of the other. If two parties are in cooperation with each other (2 above) but unequally, the one who is being cooperated with most is the benevolent exploiter of the other. This occurs when one nation is attempting to help a less developed nation develop. Both may benefit, but one more than the other. Normal exploitation takes place when one party, A, is in cooperation with the other, B, but the other, B, is in conflict with the first, A (3 above). This was exemplified in the master-slave relationship.

In economic competition the conflict between competing suppliers of a product is supposed to serve the interests of the consumer. Regulation of such competition—for example, the prohibition of price-fixing—consists of the rules that are intended to assure the cooperative aspect of the conflict.

Conflict and cooperation are measurable. Both involve the probability of achieving an objective. Therefore, even exploitation is measurable. The degree of exploitation is the difference in the probabilities of success of the parties involved. Conflict is represented by negative probabilities.

Consultant versus Educator

A consultant is one who has a bag of alleged solutions to problems facing those who have responsibility for doing something about them. The solutions may or may not work. Many are popular panaceas or practices in good currency.

They are often fads with relatively short lives.

A patient consults with (seeks the advice of) a physician.

Consultants are frequently accused of providing decision makers with solutions that they, the decision makers, want to hear. That is, consultants are used to authenticate "solutions" accepted before hand by the decision maker.

Educators attempt to provide the relevant decision makers with a way of dealing effectively with (finding a solution to) the problems they face. They come armed with methods, techniques, and procedures for solving problems; not solutions. They often participate in the application of the methods they propose, but they never use them independently of the decision makers. They believe the decision makers must participate in the decision-making process (see also EDUCATOR VERSUS GURU, pages 42-43).

Obviously, breakthrough and creative solutions to problems are more likely to be obtained by use of educators than consultants.

CORRELATION VERSUS CAUSALITY

Correlation is a measure of association between two or more variables. Two variables that tend to increase or decrease together are said to be positively correlated. Two variables such that when one increases, the other decreases are said to be negatively correlated.

For example, education and income are positively correlated. On the other hand, the more education one has the less is the number of days lost due to illness.

Correlation is not a measure of either causality or production. Recall that a cause is sufficient for its effect and a producer is necessary but not sufficient for its product. The fact that a variable is correlated with another is not sufficient basis for assuming that that variable is either the cause or the producer of the other. It may be, but correlation does not prove it.

To establish that two things tend to change or occur together is not to establish that one is the cause or producer of the other. For example, people usually brush their teeth before they go to sleep. However, brushing one's teeth is neither the cause nor the producer of going to sleep. To take another example, in one large city it was discovered that people who live in neighborhoods with a great deal of soot-fall were more likely to get tuberculosis than those who live in neighborhoods with less soot-fall. Some researchers erroneously concluded that soot was a producer of tuberculosis. Subsequent research showed that it was neither necessary nor sufficient for tuberculosis. It showed that the more soot-fall in a neighborhood, the lower the cost of housing in that neighborhood tended to be. The lower the cost of housing the poorer its inhabitants tended to be. The poorer people were, the more critically deficient their diets were. Dietary deficiencies were found to be a producer of tuberculosis not soot.

Despite its common misuses correlation can play an important role in science, in the elimination of irrelevant (uncorrelated) variables from consideration. Because causally and production—related variables must be correlated, if two variables are not correlated they can be assumed not to be related in either of these two ways.

Correlation has another important use: in prediction. The value of one of two correlated variables may be quite easy to determine while the other is difficult. Then the one that is easy to determine can be used to predict the value of the one that is difficult. For example, the amount of education a person has and his/her income are correlated. Therefore, if in a given situation education may be easier to determine than income, it can be used to predict a person's income.

One of two correlated variables may occur before the other. In those cases, the one that occurs earlier can be used to predict the other. For example, currently an increase in the cost of a barrel of oil can be used to predict what will happen in the stock market. When the price of oil goes up the market will generally go down.

There are two common misuses of correlation in addition to incorrectly inferring causality or production from it. First, an estimated correlation coefficient—one based on a random sample—will seldom be zero. This does not mean that the true coefficient is not zero. Therefore, the hypothesis that the true coefficient is zero should always be tested.

Second, correlation analysis presupposes a random sample from a well defined population. When applied to data obtained in any other way, it may not provide an appropriate basis for inference to the population from which the data were drawn. For example, among a group of patients in a particular hospital it was found that most of those who suffered from stomach ulcers were not the first born in their families. From this fact it was incorrectly inferred that first born are less likely to get stomach ulcers. A sample from a well defined larger population showed exactly the opposite: first born were more likely to get the ulcers than those later born.

CREATE VERSUS INNOVATE

To create is to produce a product, a service or a process that, to the best of the creator's knowledge, has never been produced before. The thing created may have been created by someone else at an earlier time but the current creator is unaware of this. This is sometimes referred to as "reinventing the wheel".

A creative act involves three steps:

1.   Identify a self-imposed constraint (an assumption) that limits the number of alternatives that the creator can consider.

2.   Negate that assumption and assume the contradictory is true.

3.   Explore the consequences of the negation.

These three steps can be observed in the solution of a puzzle. A puzzle differs from a problem in that the one confronted with a puzzle normally makes an assumption unconsciously that precludes discovery of a solution. For example, consider the familiar (to many) nine-dot problem. Nine dots are drawn so as to form a square. The task is to draw a straight line without lifting one's pen or pencil from the paper and cover all nine dots. The self-imposed constraint most often assumed is that one cannot go outside the boundaries of the square. When one identifies this constraint and removes it, a solution can be found. In addition, solutions can be found by folding the paper and using a felt-tipped pen.

The production of a joke is a creative act. The punch line in every joke is one that is not expected because of assumptions the listener makes. For example, a visitor to an elderly long-married couple is impressed by the fact that the husband always addresses his wife as "dear" or "honey". One assumes this is an indicator of lingering affection. However, when the visitor remarks on this to the husband when his wife is not present, the husband says, "I have to. I can't remember her name".

The product of an innovative act may be either good or bad. Not all acts of creativity are beneficial or satisfying. For example, a newly designed article of clothing may actually be repulsive to potential users. Many new products fail in the market place.

To innovate is to do something differently than it has been done before but where that thing has been done before by someone else and the innovator is aware of this fact. For example, today when an automated checkout is introduced in a supermarket, it is an innovation. Others have already introduced automated checkouts, and the innovator is aware of this. Therefore, an innovation is an adoption of a creative solution produced by another of which the innovator is aware.

In business, innovation enables a company to keep up with its competition: for example, the use of best practices. Creativity enables it to move ahead of the competition.

Customer versus Consumer

A customer is one who pays for a product or service. S/he may or may not be the consumer of that product or service. For example, one who buys a gift for another is the customer. The one who receives the gift is the consumer. A consumer is the one who uses the product or service.

If the person who receives a gift gives it to someone else, the someone else is the consumer providing s/he uses it.

Unless a product or service satisfies a need or desire of consumers, it will not succeed in the market place. But to become available it may have to be acceptable to intermediaries (e.g. wholesalers and retailers) who purchase it before selling it. They tend to serve in this role for products and services that promise to be attractive to other customers and consumers.

Products and services that are consumed by customers must appeal primarily to consumers. Products and services that are seldom purchased by the consumer must have a primary appeal to the customer, for example, food for young children or such gift items as Rolex watches and Mont Blanc pens.

Debates versus Arguments

A debate is an argument that follows rules. Despite the rules, a debate may not settle a disagreement; it may strengthen it. The parties of a debate may leave it without changed opinions or attitudes, but with new arguments for their position. However, debates can be made more productive by following the following unconventional rules.

- First, each party states his/her position as clearly as s/he can.

- Second, each party must state the opponent's position in a way that the opponent accepts.

- Third, each opponent must state the conditions under which they think the other's position would be the correct one.

- Fourth, they then discuss the nature of the current conditions.

  - If they agree on these, either the correct position is indicated, or neither position is shown to be correct.

  - If neither is shown to be correct they should reformulate their positions and start over again.

  - If they disagree, they then discuss the situation until agreement is reached or they agree on selection of a third party to settle the difference.

- Fifth, when the third party defines the current situation, this either indicates which of the two positions is correct, or, if it doesn't, they return to step four and continue until either one of the two positions is validated, or neither is.

  – If neither is validated the opponents must reformulate their positions. If they agree, this ends the process. If not, they should start over again.

This procedure places quite a burden on the opponents. Therefore, it helps to have an agreed-upon facilitator and referee run the exchanges. Of course, the opponents may never reach agreement. However, even when this is the case, the opponents will begin to understand better the nature of their disagreement.

Democracy versus Autocracy

Democracy—autocracy in their pure forms are at the two ends of a scale descriptive of the political character of a state. Real states are seldom, if ever, at the ends of the scale. However, many are near them.

A democratic state has three properties:

1.   All those members of the state who are capable and are directly affected by a decision can participate in it directly or indirectly through representatives whom they select.

     Those who elect representatives can undo any decision the representatives make. Every government decision is ultimately subject to a referendum of members of the governed society.

     It should be noted that with modern electronic technology referenda can be conducted quickly, accurately, and inexpensively.

2.   Every elected official of the state who has authority over others is subject to the collective will of those who elected them. (They can remove any elected official from office.)

     In an ideal democracy government is organized "lowerarchically", not hierarchically. All appointments and dismissals would require approval of those who will become, or are, the appointee's subordinates.

3. Every member of the state can do whatever they want provided it does not affect others or the others affected approve of the action. (This means that there are no victimless crimes in this state.)

States called democratic tend to satisfy the first and second condition fully or almost so. Few satisfy the third condition to the same extent. Many of these legislate against victimless crimes in the name of morality.

An autocratic state is one in which an individual or group can reverse any decision made by either a group or an individual within or outside the government. Most autocracies grant individuals some freedom from such oversight.

In a democracy, government exists to serve its members; in an autocracy individuals exist to serve the government and the state it governs. The fact that in a democracy government exists to serve its members implies that its members have certain specifiable obligations to it; for example, to pay taxes, obey its laws and regulations, and participate in decision making. To the extent that those who have a right to participate directly or indirectly in government decision making do not exercise that right, this is considered a shortcoming of that government as well as of the non-participants. In many cases the failure to participate, particularly in elections, follows from the fact that the non-participants believe there is no significant difference between the alternatives from which they are asked to choose.

Followers of a democratic leader do so voluntarily. In an autocracy those who have followers are usually commanders whose followers have no acceptable alternative to following them. Nor do the followers have any power over their alleged leaders. They cannot even refuse to follow, as they can in a democracy.

In a democracy the rights of every minority are protected. Not so in an autocracy. Persecution of minorities defined by ethnicity, religion, political views or sex is commonplace.

There are a number of organizations within a democracy—such as hospitals, schools, religions, and corporations—that are managed autocratically. Conversely, there are a number of organizations in an autocracy that may be managed democratically—such as professional societies, clubs, and schools.

Determinate versus Animate versus Social versus Ecological Systems

There are many different ways of classifying systems but the following is the one I have found most useful. (This does not apply to all others in the field.) For me the critical variable differentiating the types of systems is choice because without choice there can be no purposes.

Determinate systems can make no choices nor can their parts. Mechanical systems like clocks and radios are examples. Their behavior and that of their parts are completely determined by their structure, program, and environment.

Animate systems can display choices, but their parts can't. Therefore, the whole can display purposes but the parts cannot. Human beings and more developed animals are examples. Nevertheless, parts of persons or dogs and cats—for example, brain, heart and lungs—do not have choices. Their behavior is determined. Systems called organismic can be either deterministic or animate, for example, plants and animals. Animate systems can also display determined behavior as in reflex actions.

Social systems can display choice, hence purpose, and so can their parts (e.g. human beings). These are the least determined systems and therefore their futures are the most difficult to predict.

Ecological systems cannot display choice as a whole but their parts—human and social systems—can. The behavior of the whole is determined, but not some of the behavior of its parts. However, effects of the behavior of the parts on the whole are determined.

There are models of each of these types of system. Unfortunately, these models are applied not only to the type of system they represent but to other types. For example: some systems thinkers have applied deterministic models to human and social systems. Others have applied animate models to social systems.

In reverse, social systems and animate models have been applied to deterministic systems. Wherever there is a mismatch between the type of system and the type of model applied to it—and this is done frequently—false conclusions about the system are extracted and very important truths are missed.

Development versus Growth

Development and growth are not the same thing. They do not even have to interact. A person, society or thing can grow without developing—for example, a cemetery or a rubbish heap. A person or a society can develop without growing. A thing cannot develop because development involves choice of behavior and purposefulness—for example, Einstein in his later years continued to develop even though he was contracting physically.

Growth is an increase in size or number. Therefore, a child grows into an adult and the population of the United States grows as does its economy.

- Development is an increase in the desire and ability to satisfy one's needs and legitimate desires and those of others.

- A desire is legitimate if it does not decrease anyone else's ability or desire to satisfy his/her needs and desires.

Legitimate is a relative concept. What is legitimate in the United States may not be legitimate in another country. For example, freedom of religion applies in the United States but not in some Muslim countries. In the United States a woman raped is considered to be a victim but in some Muslim countries she is considered to be the perpetrator of a crime. Therefore, "legitimate" is a moral concept and this, as we will see, is relative to a society in which it is applied.

Development is an increase in competence and competence increases as a result of learning. Since no one can learn for another, no one can develop for another. The only kind of development of a person that is possible is self-development. Although one person (for example, a parent) cannot develop for another (for example, a child), one can facilitate and encourage the learning—hence the development—of another.

An ability to solve all needs and desires (which to coin a word is omnicompetence) is an ideal that can never be attained but can be approached indefinitely. Thus this ultimate objective is also ultimate means. It is necessarily an ideal for all mankind, past, present, and future, because one cannot desire anything without wanting the ability to obtain it. This is true even if what one desires is the lack of all desire, Nirvana. Omnicompetence, then, is the ideal pursued by development.

The difference between a "need" and a "desire" should also be noted. A need has as its object something that is necessary for survival, such as oxygen, food, and rest. One may not desire something that is needed because, for example, one is unaware of the need; a need for calcium or vitamin D. One may desire many things that one does not need: an automobile, a television set, gourmet food, a million dollars and so on.

Charity is frequently confused with development. For example, together with colleagues we received funds from the Secretary of the Presidency of Mexico to conduct a development effort with a remote Indian village in the Sierra Madre Mountains. The village contained about 375 families. The initial meeting was held in the town square, the zocolo, attended by most of the adults in the community. We explained what the project was about, including a definition of development. When our introduction was over one of the elders suggested we divide the money we had available for the project (approximately $40,000) evenly among the families in the village, and go home. We explained that doing so was not development but charity. In explaining the difference we referred to a familiar Chinese proverb: when a hungry man is given a fish, he will be hungry again tomorrow. But if you teach him how to fish, he will never be hungry again. The attendees then began to explore the meaning of development by asking questions. The first two expenditures authorized were the purchase of a bullock to pull the plow used in their agricultural activities and the transportation of water into the community from the nearest well which was four kilometers from the village. Both of these acts enabled the community to use what it knew in a better way than previously in satisfying both its needs and desires.

Misunderstanding of the difference between development and charity is characteristic of almost all national and supranational (UN, World Bank and IMF) so-called development programs directed at those regions or countries that are less developed. After more than fifty years I can think of no conspicuous example of development that any of these agencies or others of the same type have accomplished as a result of their support.

Successful facilitation of neighborhood development has revealed principles that are applicable to all development assistance efforts. These are:

- Do not pretend to know how (1) to develop the targeted society or (2) even to learn how to do so.

- Offer yourself as a resource that the targeted society must learn how to use by trial and error.

- All projects within the program must be directed at development of the society or some of its members, not at charity.

- All decisions about the nature of the development projects should be made democratically within the relevant community, region or nation.

- Absolutely no corruption should be tolerated. If it is observed within the program, the program will be discontinued immediately.

DISCIPLINES VERSUS SUBJECTS

Our educational system leads us to believe without question that problems and subjects fall into different disciplines. We do not question that there are physical problems, chemical problems, biological problems, economic problems, political problems, management problems, and so on and on. But there are no such things.

The adjectives before the word problem tells us absolutely nothing about the problem. They tell us something, but not about the problem. It is easiest to grasp this truth by example. Just north of the University of Pennsylvania is an area, Mantua, that was once called an urban black ghetto. Fortunately a small group of faculty members began to collaborate with community leaders helping in any way they were asked to. About six faculty members and an equal number of community activists met every Monday morning in one of the professor's offices. During these meetings the professors were assigned new tasks, and their progress on old ones was reviewed. During one of these meetings a young man from the community broke in with very disturbing news.

An 83-year-old woman who lived in the neighborhood and had led a group in development efforts had died that morning. She was returning home from her monthly health checkup at a neighborhood clinic. She had a defective heart. She had been tested and told she was OK. While climbing the stairs to reach her rooms on the fourth floor of a big old house in which she lived she had had a heart attack and died.

The news stopped our meeting. The first one to speak, after a lull, was a professor of public health. He said: "I told you we need more doctors in the clinic. If we had more, we could make house calls and if we had made a house call to her, this never would have happened." After another pause the professor of economics spoke up: "There are plenty of doctors but they are private practitioners and she could not afford one. If her welfare payments had been larger or if we had an adequate national healthcare plan, this never would have happened." Another pause followed, broken by a professor of architecture. He said: "Why don't we require elevators in buildings like that?" This too would obviously have prevented the death.

Then the only woman present, a professor of social work, spoke up: "You don't know anything about that woman. She was married as a teenager and shortly thereafter gave birth to a son. Unfortunately, she was simultaneously abandoned by her husband whom she never saw again. She took loving care of the boy and supported him by doing menial housework. The son was brilliant. When he graduated from high school he earned a scholarship to the University of Pennsylvania. He graduated from there *cum summa laude*, and got a scholarship from the Law School. He distinguished himself there and got a job with one of the largest law firms in Philadelphia. He is now in his forties, a senior partner in that firm, is married, and with his two children lives in a beautiful home in the suburbs that is all on one floor. If the old lady and her son were not alienated from each other she would be living with him where she would have all the money she needed and no steps to climb."

What kind of a problem was her death: medical, economic, architectural, or social work? None, or what is equivalent, all of them. The disciplinary adjectives in front of "problem" tell us the point of view of the person looking at the problem, nothing about the problem.

Most problems can be approached in many different disciplinary ways. Even if most could yield solutions they are not all equal. Some give a bigger "bang for the buck" than others. It is better to take an aspirin to cure a headache than submit to brain surgery.

Every problem should be looked at from as many different disciplinary perspectives as possible. Only in this way can the "best possible" approach to it be found.

Downsizing versus Rightsizing

Downsizing consists of ending the employment of full-time employees and sometimes replacing them with temporary employees. This reduces not only the compensation of full-time employees, but it also reduces benefit costs associated with full-time employment since temporary employees receive no such benefits.

Rightsizing is often used as a synonym for "downsizing" because it appears to remove some of the onus attached to laying employees off. This is a self-serving deception. The term should be applicable to the addition of employees, but it seldom is.

A number of studies have shown that, in most cases, downsizing does not decrease costs of operation for more than a very few years. There are several reasons for this. Downsizing is usually accompanied by an enticing offer to those who are willing to leave the company voluntarily. This is most attractive to the most competent employees because they believe they can more easily find other employment than the less competent workers. Therefore, it often later requires hiring expensive consultants to fill in for lost competence. Downsizing also often has negative effects on the morale of retained employees and reduces their productivity.

From society's point of view downsizing is dysfunctional, if not immoral. Business enterprises, like all systems, have a function in the larger systems of which they are a part: society. Companies and corporations have a responsibility to society for providing productive employment. This is the only means available to a capitalist society for simultaneously producing and distributing wealth. Business enterprises distribute wealth in a number of ways: employee compensation, dividends, interest on loans, investing in other firms, and so on. All other means of distributing wealth do not produce it. Therefore, from society's point of view it may even be considered to be counter productive.

Even more important is the fact that downsizing is often unnecessary. This does <u>not</u> mean an enterprise should keep unproductive employees, but it means it should find productive employment for them, either inside or outside the enterprise. This can almost always be done by a caring and thoughtful executive. For example, James Rinehart (now deceased) the former CEO of Clarke Equipment Corporation, took the executive position at Clarke when it was in a serious financial state. Rinehart found that one of the causes was the excessive cost of transporting equipment produced by Clarke (i.e. forklift trucks and mobile construction equipment) to its widely dispersed distributors. He also found the company would save considerable money by using commercial carriers.

Rinehart found that laying off the 450 workers involved in internally provided transportation would involve considerable costs. He saw that the total amount would go a long way toward a leveraged buyout of the transportation department and all its equipment. He sought and found the promise of the additional capital required from local banks. He then presented the possibility of such a buyout to the department's employees. If they took it, he said, he would guarantee them all of Clarke's transportation of heavy equipment for two years providing they offered the same price as was offered by other commercial carriers. They took it.

Today it is a thriving trucking company. No one lost employment and Clarke got less expensive transportation in return. Employment can often be found or created outside the enterprise involved. But it requires a thoughtful and socially committed executive to do so and there are not many with this combination of characteristics.

Educator versus Guru

A guru produces a doctrine and disciples. S/he identifies the questions and answers that are permissible. Therefore s/he discourages any independent thought in his/her disciples. Their task is to disseminate the doctrine and attract other disciples.

An educator tries to induce learning, including encouraging the asking of questions and finding answers to them. The educator tries to stimulate independent thinking among his/her students.

When a guru asks a question of a disciple s/he expects the answer that he has previously provided. When an educator asks a question of a student s/he hopes for an answer that s/he does not expect but which is nevertheless correct. Educators encourage creativity, skepticism, and intellectual explorations. Gurus encourage compliance and conformity.

The American anthropologist Jules Henry asked what would follow if, "all through school the young were provoked to question the Ten Commandments, the sanctity of revealed religion, the foundations of patriotism, the profit motive, the two party system, monogamy, the laws of incest, and so on..." (p. 288 in *Culture against Man*, Random House, New York, 1963). Ronald Laing, a prominent British psychiatrist, answered that there would be more creativity than society could handle, but not more than it should be capable of handling (pp. 71-72 in *The Politics of Experience*, Ballantine Books, New York, 1967).

Gurus take themselves to be infallible and have few if any doubts about the doctrines they espouse. Educators, on the other hand, are doubtful about many of their beliefs.

In most schools teachers are more like gurus than educators.

Management Guru dispensing doctrine

Equal versus Equality

Despite our founding fathers it is apparent that all "men" (let alone women) were not created equal. However, they did not mean that all those born are equal at birth but that they are entitled to equal opportunity to satisfy their needs and desires: equality. Equality would prevail in a society in which there were no correlation between the socio-economic characteristics of children and their parents. This means, for example, there would be no inheritance of poverty, class, or ignorance. All would have an equal chance to realize the "American dream".

Of course there have been efforts to show that there are differences in endowed abilities in different races, particularly between African Americans and white Americans. But these and similarly alleged researches have uniformly been shown to be wrong.

It is apparent that although significant progress toward equality has been made in our society, we are still a long way from attaining it. Furthermore, it differs widely from community to community and neighborhood to neighborhood. Race, sex, and ethnicity (all inherited characteristics) still can significantly reduce chances for self-fulfillment.

Errors of Commission versus Errors of Omission

There are two kinds of mistake: errors of commission and errors of omission. Errors of commission consist of doing something that should not have been done. Errors of omission consist of not doing something that should have been done. In general, errors of omission—which include lost opportunities—tend to be more serious than errors of commission. They are usually either very difficult or impossible to correct.

For example, when Eastman Kodak bought Sterling Drug—an error of commission—it eventually had to unload it at a considerable cost. It did not have the competence to conduct a pharmaceutical business.

When Kodak failed to take digital photography seriously while the Japanese were doing so, a much more serious mistake was made for which it will be paying (as lost income) for a very long time.

All through school students are punished for making mistakes, usually errors of commission. The punishment usually consists of lowering a grade. Therefore, to the extent possible, students try to avoid mistakes, even cheating if necessary to do so.

Schools seldom recognize the simple fact that one does not learn by doing something right. All that one can derive from doing something right is confirmation of what one already knows. This has some value but not as much as what one can learn from identifying and correcting mistakes. Nevertheless, schools give little opportunity for such learning. For example, examinations are not given again after having been returned to students to see if they have corrected the mistakes they made in the first examination, hence, if they have learned.

When students graduate and go to work in an organization of any kind they usually find that mistakes are also frowned upon there and, therefore, are to be avoided. Where a mistake cannot be avoided an effort is made to arrange for responsibility for it to be transferred to another. One is often punished for making a mistake, varying from a verbal reprimand to demotion or firing. But accounting systems almost universally record only errors of commission for which a cost can usually be determined with relative ease. They do not record more serious errors of omission because these are much more difficult to place a cost on.

Therefore, to maximize job security one must either avoid errors of commission or arrange for someone else to receive blame for them. One need not worry so much about errors of omission because these are not recorded. The way to maximize security is to do as little as possible. It is the imbalance between the ways errors are handled that makes for conservative management in every kind of organization. This is as true in government as in for-profit and non-profit organizations.

Ethics versus Morality

Ethics consists of universally applicable principles of behavior that differentiate good and evil.

Morality consists of society-relevant principles of behavior that differentiate between right and wrong.

Moral principles differ from country to country. The treatment of women is a conspicuous example. The treatment of religious freedom is another. On the other hand, a principle such as "Don't do unto others as you would not have them to unto you" is supposed to hold universally. Unfortunately, extreme terrorists do not behave towards their enemies in accordance with this rule.

Some argue that there are no universal principles of good behavior. This is because they do not recognize a universal desire of all mankind, past, present, and future. As previously noted, there is such a desire: to be able to satisfy one's desires. One cannot desire anything without desiring the ability required to obtain it, even Nirvana. This is equivalent to the childhood wish that all one's wishes would come true. The ability to fulfill all one's desires is seldom if ever attainable and, therefore, is an ideal. This ideal implies that it is universally "good" to enhance another's ability to satisfy their desires, but only those desires that, if satisfied, do not reduce anyone's ability to obtain theirs. This implies that to increase another's ability to obtain his/her legitimate objectives is good. To reduce this ability is evil.

Fact versus Law versus Theory

One statement is more general than another if the first implies the second. For example, "All living human beings have a brain" is more general than, "Bill Clinton has a brain." In addition, a statement that holds true over a larger set of environments than another can be said to be more general than the other. For example, "A hermetically sealed clock will work in any environment" is more general than, "This clock will work in this environment."

The less general a statement is, the more fact-like it is. The more general a statement is the more law-like it is. However, there is not a very sharp distinction between a fact and law, nor between a law and a theory.

A theory is even more general than a law; it implies laws. Newton's theory of gravitation implied many other laws discovered both before and after his discovery.

The differences between a fact, law, and theory are most easily seen in a deductive system like Euclidean geometry. This geometry consists of four parts: (1) a set of undefined and defined concepts, (2) a set of assumptions (axioms and postulates), (3) a set of deduced theorems, and (4) instances of the theorems. The assumptions constitute a theory. The theorems are laws. The instances of the theorems are facts.

Theories are also expected to suggest and lead to new laws. They are also thought by many to be more difficult to confirm than laws, and laws more difficult to confirm than facts. But this is not the case. The difficulty of confirmation is more dependent on the seriousness of the possible errors than on the generality of the statement being tested. The difficulty of confirming a factual statement such as "A specified thing is red" depends on the cost of an error in making such a determination. If a life depends on it, confirmation is much more difficult than if the observation is casual. On the other hand, a theory whose consequences are unimportant may be very easy to confirm.

There have been many historical instances in which a fact that was inconsistent with a theory was not used to discard the theory, but to raise questions about the validity of the fact. It is just as true that theories can call the truth of a fact into question as that facts can call the validity of a theory into question. To use a metaphor, fact, law, and theory do not form a line, but rather a circle with mutual dependencies; they are interdependent (see also INDUCTION VERSUS DEDUCTION, pages 64-65).

FEDERATION VERSUS CONFEDERATION

A federation is an alliance between (a union of) social entities
(e.g. states or nations) with a centralized management/
government whose laws and regulations take precedence over
those made by its members. The United States is a federation of
states. No state in the union can legislate or regulate in a way that
is not consistent with decisions and policies made by the federal
government. Each state, in turn, is a federation of the counties,
townships, and cities within it.

A confederation is an alliance between (a union of) social entities
(e.g. states or nations) with a centralized management that cannot
overrule any law or regulation made by one of its members. The
authorities of the center are given to it by its members and can
therefore be revoked by its members. Each part of the alliance
has the right of withdrawal from it. The United Nations is an
example of a confederation.

In effect, a federation is a hierarchy (authority and resources flow
down) and a confederation is a "lowerarchy" (authority and
resources flow up).

Forecast versus Predict

A forecast is a statement of an expected future based on a projection of what has happened and is happening now. Weather is forecasted. Given the weather patterns of the last few days and today a projection is made of what it is likely to be for the next few days. Forecasts are statistical in nature. Regression analysis is often used as the method of projecting the future.

A prediction is a statement of an expected future that is not based on data but on beliefs about that which is predicted and its causes or producers. For example, to say at the beginning of a football season which team one expects to win the Super Bowl is a prediction. Near the end of the season the final position of the teams can be forecasted based on their earlier performance. There may be contradictory predictions, for example, of who will be the next president of the United States. Those who foresee a war with Iran are making a prediction but so are those who don't. Prediction can be about things that have never happened in the past. Not so for forecasts.

The trip to the moon was based on a number of predictions that were drawn from physical theories. On the other hand, the probability that a bomb dropped from an airplane will hit a specified target can be forecasted based on a statistical analysis of past droppings.

Prediction can be derived from knowledge of how something works. For example, we can predict that without gasoline an automobile will not run. We can do this without ever having observed an instance of a car running out of gas.

Since forecasts are projected from data, conflicting forecasts of the same thing are less likely than prediction of the same thing. Different weather forecasters may differ in their forecasts but the differences are not likely to be large. Differences among predictions can be large. Of course there are situations where projections from past data can lead to different forecasts as in picking the winners of horse races.

We predict that someone will pick up a one hundred dollar bill dropped on a sidewalk. This is not based on data but on what we believe about the nature of people. It is an inference drawn from an assumption about the nature of people.

In science a prediction of a future event can be inferred from a law or a theory. To the extent that the predictions extracted from a law or theory are correct, the law or theory is considered to be confirmed. If such predictions are false, either the law or theory is taken to be disconfirmed or the validity of the events that did not meet predictions are questioned.

To a very large extent our futures are determined by what we do between now and then. Therefore, to a significant extent we can bring about a relevant (to us) part of the future. The best way to predict the future is to make it happen. There are aspects of the future that we can control; for example, where we live, what work we do, and who we will spend time with. In general we can control either causes or effects. For example, we can prevent the mosquitoes that bear yellow fever from coming or we can inoculate people against yellow fever. Where we can't control what will happen, we can often identify the possibilities and prepare for each and be ready for them. This is called contingency planning. Or we can become flexible—ready, willing and able to change as conditions around us change—that is, we can be adaptive. We get to our destination driving our automobile by responding rapidly and effectively to the actions of other drivers and weather conditions.

From Data to Wisdom

There are five types of content in the human mind: data, information, knowledge, understanding, and wisdom. They form a hierarchy: information is more valuable than data, knowledge more valuable than information, understanding more valuable than knowledge, and wisdom more valuable than understanding. Nevertheless schools and organizations of all types tend to focus on the lower-valued aspects of mental content (especially information) rather than on the more highly valued understanding and wisdom.

Data consists of symbols that represent properties of objects and events. For example, street addresses designate locations using numeric and alphabetic symbols. Inventories consist of numbers attached to various items identified alphabetically. These too are data.

Information consists of data that have been processed to be useful. They are related much as iron ore is to iron. Very little can be done with iron ore (data) but once it is converted to iron (information) it has very many uses.

Information is contained in descriptions, answers to questions that begin with words such as who, what, when, and how many.

Knowledge as know-how is contained in instructions, answers to questions that begin with "how to". It is one thing to know in what city some activity is located—information—but another to know how to get there—knowledge. It is one thing to know that an automobile can carry you from one place to another—information—but another to know how to drive one—knowledge.

It is yet another matter to know why a person wants to go there. Explanations are contained in answers to questions beginning with why. They provide understanding.

Data, information, knowledge, and understanding all can contribute to the efficiency with which we can pursue objectives; with whether we do things right.

Wisdom, on the other hand, is concerned with effectiveness, whether we do the right thing. Wisdom is contained in evaluations. It provides a person with a willingness to make short-term sacrifices in order to make longer-term gains.

There is a significant difference between doing something right and doing the right thing. The more efficiently we do the wrong thing, the "wronger" we become. When we correct an error committed in pursuing the wrong thing, we become "wronger". If we commit an error doing the right thing and correct it we become "righter". Therefore, it is better to do the right thing wrong and correct it than to do the wrong thing right.

Function versus Purpose

A thing's function is the use to which it can be put or can put itself. The function of an automobile, for example, is to carry people and goods from one place to another under a person's control, in privacy, and on land. The function of a meeting's chairman is to call the meeting to order, see that it proceeds according to its rules of order, and to close the meeting.

Any object, living or not, can have one or more functions. For example, a screwdriver can be used to turn screws or pry a lid off a can. A person can have many functions, for example, parent, lawyer, tennis player, and so on.

A thing has a purpose if it can produce an outcome in different ways in the same and different environments. For example, one person can have communication with another as his/her purpose if s/he uses either a telephone, a computer, or a hand-written letter to communicate with that other person and does so in different environments.

To have a purpose, something must be capable of making choices. This is not required to have a function. There are many things— for example, inanimate tools like hammer and saws—that have functions but not purposes. However, things, like people, that have purposes can also have many functions.

For a thing to have a function it must have a potential or actual user, even if the user is the thing itself. For example, hammers and saws have carpenters as users. But a person can use him/ herself to nail two pieces of wood together. One person can use another to do this. A corporation has a function: to produce and distribute wealth. In this case society is the user. Corporations are instruments of society. Since they can make choices they also have purposes: e.g. to satisfy customers and to make a profit.

It is the way a user uses a thing that determines what its functions are. For example, a clock may be used to tell time and also as a paper weight. If thrown at someone, it can also be used as a weapon. It is the user of a thing that has a function that is responsible for its use. Thus the driver of an automobile is responsible for safe driving. A car may cause an accident because of a part's failure, but the automobile is not responsible for that accident. The maker of the car who used a defective part is. Questions of responsibility for accidents and failures easily become public issues. For example, handguns have the function of killing people, but they do not choose to do so. A shooter does. Therefore, some argue that the misuse of guns, like the misuse of automobiles, is the user's fault not that of the manufacturer of the instrument. Nevertheless, the absence of a misused instrument would, of course, prevent it being misused. This would also preclude its being used properly.

Guide versus Coach

A guide is someone who shows others the way to reach a particular destination that the others want to reach. It may be a way to a place—for example, a library—or to an object such as a book in a library. Each of us often requests guidance; for example, when we ask the way to a restroom, or to particular department in a department store, or to the bottom of the Grand Canyon.

A coach is someone who enables other human beings to do something (usually engage in a competitive activity) they want to do more effectively. This is why athletic teams and even individual competitive athletes have coaches. The objective of those being coached is always to do better in the type of competition for which they are being coached.

A trainer is someone who enables animate others to reach a physical condition in which they can engage in a particular activity more effectively. One can train horses, dogs, and many other animals as well as human beings, but one does not coach the other animals. To be coached, one must be able to make choices.

To facilitate is to enable others to do anything better then they would without such help. To facilitate the learning of a subject matter by another is to tutor that other.

Hear versus Listen

To hear something is to perceive a sound of any type. To listen to it is to pay attention to it. One frequently hears things to which one pays no attention, even speech. For example, students attending a class in which a teacher is lecturing may "turn the teacher off"—that is, hear the teacher but not listen to him or her. One must hear something in order to listen to it. A listener may not get a message intended or may receive a message not intended. This is apparent when politics are involved.

Different people may listen to the same speaker and take different meanings from it. Again, this is particularly true where politics is involved. What one hears when listening may vary considerably depending on the beliefs and attitudes brought to the hearing experience.

To see and notice differ in the same way as to hear and listen. Those who see the same thing may differ in what they notice depending also on what they bring to the experience.

Hierarchy versus "Lowerarchy"

A hierarchy is an organization in which the Chief Executive Officer (CEO) can reject any decision made, or work done, by any employee of the organization. S/he is also the ultimate source of all resources used within the organization. Any other manager can do the same but only for their subordinates. Therefore, in a hierarchy, authority and resources flow down from the top, all the way to the bottom.

A "lowerarchy" (a term not to be found in a dictionary) is an organization in which all authority and resources flow from the bottom up. Approval of decision and work must be obtained from subordinates not superiors.

In general, military organizations are the most severely hierarchical. This is reflected in the fact that the person at the top of a military unit is called a "commander" as well as "chief".

In principle, a democracy is supposed to be a lowerarchy, but few if any are. Most including ours operate as a hierarchy with very few exceptions. The ability of the electorate to recall an elected official or have a person in a position of authority impeached is a lowerarchical (but seldom used) capability.

Professional societies tend to be lowerarchical.

There are some businesses and schools that have become more lowerarchical than hierarchical, and with considerable success: for example, corporations such as Metalex, SAP, and Goretech and a school such as the Sudbury Valley School in Framingham, Mass.

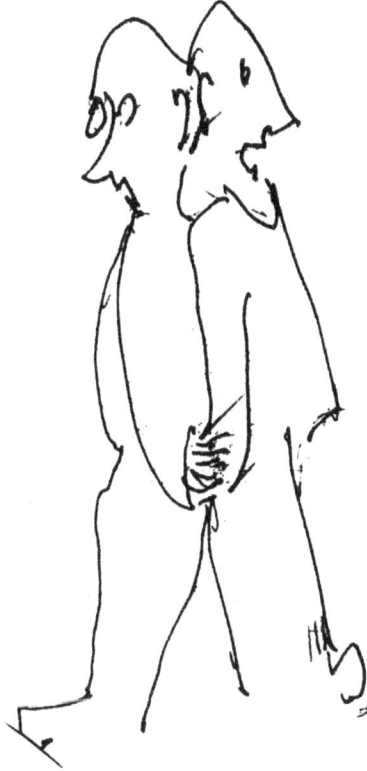

A CEO Conferring with an HR Manager

Iconic versus Analog versus Symbolic Models

A model is a representation of something. For example, the small plastic automobiles that children play with are models of real automobiles. Models of ships and airplanes are familiar objects. These, however, are only one type of model, iconic.

Iconic models are representations that have some of the same properties as the thing they represent. They usually differ in size from the real thing; are larger or smaller. But they look like the thing they depict. Photographs and painted portraits are iconic models of the person pictured. The things represented by iconic models are usually easy to identify, but difficult to change. This means they are seldom used to explore possible changes in the thing represented. But they are often used to find that which is represented.

An analog model employs properties different than those the thing represented have to represent some of its properties. Thus we can have a hydraulic model of an electrical system. In such a model the flow of water is used to represent the flow of electrical current. There are also hydraulic models of the economy in which the flow of water is used to represent the flow and disposition of money. (The Moniac is a computer-based model of a national economy.) A slide rule is an analog model in which distance represents logarithms.

The real thing represented by an analog is more difficult to identify than is the case with an iconic model. However, it is much easier to explore the effects of changes in the real thing using such a model. One can change the flows of water and the location of valves in a hydraulic model relatively easily, but not so the flow of money itself.

Finally a symbolic model uses numeric or alphabetic symbols to represent something. Mathematical models, for example, are commonly used in science. $S=\frac{1}{2}\,gt^2$ is a symbolic model of a falling body where S represents the distance covered, g represents the gravitational constant, and t represents the elapsed time of the fall. Symbolic models are more unlike the thing they represent than iconic or analog models but much easier to use in exploring the effects of changes in the real thing.

Decision models are symbolic models. For example, they represent the relevant variables that are subject to control and those that are not, together with the outcomes they produce. This makes it possible to explore the consequences of different values of the controllable and uncontrollable variables in that situation. Although the ease of manipulation increases as one goes from iconic thru analog to symbolic models, the likelihood of error in the representation generally increases.

Induction versus Deduction

Induction is a way of extracting general statements (for example, laws) from specific ones (containing data or information). When information, knowledge, and understanding are extracted from data, induction is involved. Therefore, most market and social surveys, and election polls, supply data from which generalizations about a specified population are drawn.

Induction is also a way of extracting facts from facts. From the presence of loud angry words exchanged by two people we induce that they are in disagreement about something. From the fact that a person is unusually well dressed we assume that s/he is going somewhere special, such as a party, a date, or a concert. Conversion of a set of specific observations into a general statement is commonplace. For example, if we collect information on income of college graduates in different age groups, and for non-college graduates for the same age groups, we draw the general conclusion that college graduates earn more at any given age than non-college graduates of the same age.

When we go from general statements (laws or theories) to specific ones (statements of fact) we engage in deduction. For example, when we go from our belief about income of college and non-college graduates to belief that a particular college graduate is earning more than a specific non-college graduate of the same age, we are engaged in deduction. From theories we deduce statements of fact, the truth of which is tested to determine the validity of the theory. For example, some of us believe that persons who display their "alleged" morality in public have a greater tendency to violate it in private. To react with an "I told you so" is commonplace when an evangelist or sanctimonious politician is revealed in a violation of common morality.

It is not at all uncommon to use both inductive and deductive reasoning in a single inquiry. Neither is one inherently better than the other. They are interdependent. In fact, it is not possible to collect data without making some general (law-like) assumptions. Nor is it possible to make a generalization without assuming some facts.

Intrinsic versus Extrinsic

Something has intrinsic value if it is an end in itself; it is not used as a means for getting something else. Examples are: pure entertainment, reading a novel, listening to a symphony, visiting a museum, playing a game or going to an amusement park. Something has extrinsic value if it can be used as a means to a desired outcome: for example, a computer or an automobile. Some things may have both intrinsic and extrinsic value. For example, driving an automobile may be satisfying no matter where one is going and at the same time it may take someone where s/he wants to go.

Beauty is an intrinsic value of things: for example products of any of the arts or crafts. A house or a building may be beautiful and thus be a pleasure to look at. A beautiful thing may also be useful. Production of such things is the objective of industrial designers. Automobiles are examples. There are those we think of as "beauties". Designing intrinsic value into products or services that have extrinsic value increases their appeal to customers. The Scandinavians seem to have a special talent for doing this. They are able to make the most utilitarian of objects—for example, kitchen utensils—beautiful.

Fun is also an intrinsic value of such activities as going for a hike, playing a game, watching a movie or reading a good book.

Beauty and fun are aesthetic values. Aesthetics has to do with creation and recreation. A work of art can inspire us to do something creative. Inspiration gives us the courage to try for something no matter how remote or improbable, and it makes us willing to make sacrifices in the pursuit. Recreation gives us the pauses that refresh us—to renew our determination to pursue an ideal, for example.

Instrumental value is the objective of technology. It tries to produce things that will serve a purpose: that help us in the pursuit of an objective. A thing that is instrumental relative to one objective may not be relative to others. For example, automobiles that obviously are valuable instruments for going places also produce pollution and cause congestion. Pharmaceuticals that cure one ailment can have side effects that seriously affect survival.

The objective of any product's design is to create something that is beautiful, fun to use, useful for an intended objective, and that does not have any harmful or undesirable side effects. It often takes considerable thought and effort to avoid unwanted side effects.

Introversion versus Extroversion

An introvert is one who responds more to internal than external stimuli and who tends to act on himself/herself rather than on the environment. An extrovert is the opposite, one who responds to external stimuli and who tends to act on his/her environment.

Two different scales are involved: sensitivity to self (subjectiversion) or the environment (objectiversion), and action directed to changing oneself (internalizing) or one's environment (externalizing).

It is clear then that there are four basic types:

- Introversion: subjective internalizers
- Extroversion: objective externalizers

  Mixed types:
    - Subjective externalizers and
    - Objective internalizers.

It is useful to cite some prototypical (familiar) examples of each type:

- John Wayne—Objective Externalizer, Extrovert

  In virtually all the parts played by John Wayne in motion pictures he was swept up in a cause not of his own making, but one presented to him or imposed by the environment.

In each he undertook doing something about an external situation, usually manipulating or otherwise affecting others a great deal.

- Joan of Arc—Subjective Externalizer

  She was dedicated to changing her environment but was driven to do so by an inner vision, and the voices she believed she heard (those of St. Michael, St. Catherine and St. Margaret).

- Forence Nightingale—Objective Internalizer

  She was extremely sensitive to the needs of others and dedicated herself to satisfying them, through nursing, even at considerable cost to herself.

- Vincent van Gogh—Subjective Internalizer, Introvert

  He was virtually a recluse, withdrawn from the environment and involved with his own inner feelings and reactions to his experience. His painting was directed at satisfying his own needs, not those of others. His efforts to form intimate relationships with others almost always failed. He spent much time in an asylum in solitary confinement.

The personality space these types occupy can be further divided into nine types: Subjectiverts, Objectiverts, Internalizers, Externalizers, Introverts, Extroverts, Subjective Externalizers, Objective Internalizers, and Centroverts. These are shown graphically in the chart overleaf.

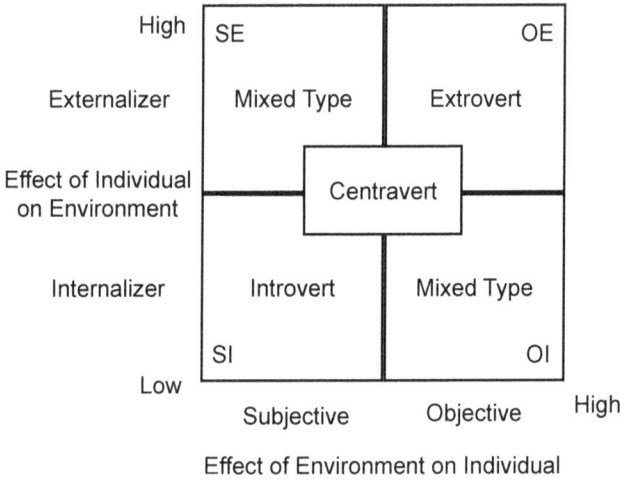

	High	SE		OE
Externalizer		Mixed Type		Extrovert
Effect of Individual on Environment			Centravert	
Internalizer		Introvert		Mixed Type
		SI		OI
	Low			

Subjective   Objective   High

Effect of Environment on Individual

Four basic types of personality

Research has revealed that different types have different product preferences; tend to attract or repel each other; and get along well or badly together. It has also been shown that different types are attracted to different types of work and are better at tasks that fit their personalities. Nuns, for example, tend to be introverted; politicians, extroverted; salesmen and radical reformers, subjective externalizers; and caring professionals, nursing and servants, objective internalizers.

These and other findings can be found in a monograph, *Exploring Personality: An Intellectual Odyssey*, by Russell L. Ackoff. CQM-INTERACT, Cambridge, MA, 1998.

MAJORITY VERSUS PLURALITY VERSUS CONSENSUS

A majority is a very familiar concept: more than half of the relevant decision makers. A minority is less than half. A plurality differs from a majority: it is the group of participants in a decision-making process who have the largest number of votes. Therefore, a group that has a plurality may or may not be a majority. The percentage of voters in a plurality may actually be quite small. The larger the number of alternatives from which a selection is to be made the greater is the chance that a majority will not be obtained and a plurality will be required to reach a decision. This is particularly apparent where the entities involved in making a decision are political parties.

Consensus is the least understood of these concepts. It is widely known that it involves complete agreement, but not on what. Consider the following incident. The CEO of a large corporation divided 72 senior managers into eight groups of nine members each. He asked each group independently to produce a redesign of their corporation. When these were completed and presented to the assembled whole, the CEO attempted to find out which one the group thought was best. None of the eight designs received votes from any members other than the ones in the group that produced it. The CEO turned to a consultant who had suggested the process and asked what he was supposed to do. There was not a majority, not even a plurality, let alone complete agreement. The consultant said that the CEO was asking the wrong question. The CEO asked the consultant to ask it.

The consultant told the group their choice was between the consultant (1) making the choice from among the eight designs and (2) doing nothing. The vote to let the consultant make the choice was unanimous; consensus was obtained. This led the group to go back to the drawing board and produce a design that the group unanimously said was as good as possible. Consensus can be on what is better rather than on what is best.

Consensus in practice, in contrast to consensus in principle, involves agreement on what is desirable to do, not necessarily on what is the best thing to do. In other words, consensus can be on a satisfactory decision, rather than on one that is optimal. Herbert Simon, the Nobel prize winning economist, called this satisficing, combining "satisfy" and "suffice".

Matrix versus Multidimensional Organizations

A matrix organization is one divided into input and output units. All personnel are assigned to one input and one output unit. An input unit is one whose output is consumed within the organization: for example, various skill groups such as those defined by the sciences or technology. An output unit is one whose output is consumed or used outside the organization: for example, units defined by product or service provided. The input units have responsibility for maintaining and increasing the skills of their members.

In a matrix organization each employee has two bosses, one from the input unit of which s/he is a member, and one from the output unit of which s/he is a member.

This structure lends itself especially to research and development organizations, where output units are thought of as defined by programs or projects. The fact that each individual has two bosses can be, and often is, a source of difficulty, if not trouble. The two bosses to whom an individual reports can place contradictory demands on him or her. This results in a type of organization-induced schizophrenia.

A multidimensional organization has, in addition to input and output units, a third type of unit, one that is defined by the class of users (markets) it tries to serve. The idea of a multidimensional organization derives from a concern over the need of most organizations to reorganize frequently. Reorganizations are costly and time consuming, and generally have a negative effect on the morale of many employees.

Reorganizations come about in an effort to adapt to changes occurring either internally or externally as, for example, in AT&T when its monopoly was destroyed and it had to compete with other organizations for the first time.

W. C. Coggin, then CEO of Dow Corning, recognized the source and nature of such reorganizations. He noted that all organizations involve a division of labor. He found that all and only three criteria are used in any type of organization for dividing labor: input units (functionally defined), output units (product- or service-defined) and category-of-user units (market-defined).

Market units may be defined either geographically (as by country or region), or by type of buyers (as retailers, and wholesalers), or by user characteristics (for example, age, sex, or occupation).

In every conventional organization there is an implicit ordering of these criteria. For example, in a monopoly, market-defined units are relatively unimportant since little marketing must be done when an organization is the sole source of a product or service, as AT&T was before it was deregulated. In an organization that makes only one type of product, functional (input) units are the most important. But in an organization that has many different products, especially, those for different markets, the output units are generally defined by the type of product produced.

Coggin observed that all major reorganizations consist of a reordering of the three criteria imbedded in the organization. Therefore, he sought a way to make such reorganizations unnecessary. The multidimensional organization is the result. It has all three types of unit at each level of the organization.

In this type of organization all personnel are assigned to an input unit. These units are skill-defined; for example, accounting, purchasing, and industrial engineering. Most individuals are assigned to one or more output or market-defined units but the heads of these units are not bosses but clients of the input units. These units assign their personnel to one or more other types of unit. Therefore, the heads of units to which personnel are assigned have complete flexibility with respect to the personnel they use. They are clients who can reject any person assigned to them, and can request anyone they would like to have work for them. Individual employees in multidimensional organizations have more control over where they are assigned than in matrix or conventional organizations. The input unit to which a person belongs receives very important personnel information from the heads of other units to which personnel are assigned.

Adaptation to changes now takes place by changing the allocation of resources to the three types of unit. If, for example, marketing becomes more important because of deregulation of an industry, more resources would be allocated to market-defined units, and less to others. Furthermore, units of any type can be added or subtracted at any time without restructuring. Restructuring is never necessary.

Means versus Ends versus Ideals

A means is behavior intended to produce a desired outcome: an end. Ends expected to be attained in the short run are frequently called goals. Those expected in a longer run are generally called objectives. An objective that can never be attained but can be approached indefinitely is called an ideal.

Means and ends are relative concepts. An end pursued in the short run—a goal—often is a means to a further-out end—an objective. A student, for example, takes a course (a means), say in production, learning about which is a goal. But that goal is itself a means to the objective of getting a degree.

I listen to a concert or watch a play (means) in order to be entertained. But entertainment is not a means to anything further. Therefore, it is referred to as "an end in itself". This is true of any end that is not a means to a more remote objective.

A popular saying asserts: the end justifies the means. This implies that a moral end justifies even an immoral means. Thus, for example, it is argued in the United States today that torture (an immoral means) is justified by the need to extract important information from captured terrorists (an objective). The negative value of the means (torture), it is further argued, is more than balanced by the positive value obtained by its use. War, considered by many to be evil, is nevertheless considered to often produce desirable ends. It is argued by some that at least in some situations, no moral means (e.g. diplomacy) can produce the same outcome. For example, when one is attacked in such a way that death is the inevitable outcome unless there is an appropriate response, one should defend oneself by any means, however immoral it may be when considered separately. There is no reason to believe this issue will be resolved in the foreseeable future.

There are those, like the Quakers, who believe that no end justifies immoral means. This is the foundation of their opposition to war. They point out that people like Dr. Martin Luther King and Mahatma Gandhi could produce major social changes without violence or other means they considered to be immoral. To expect a person to accept death rather than use, say, a violent defense is to expect saint-like behavior. The fact is that there are conditions under which everyone is willing to use an immoral means to obtain a moral end. To take a simple example, most people would consider telling a lie to save a life to be morally acceptable—as when runaway slaves were hidden by pacifists. When obtaining a very valuable end requires an immoral choice, most people would choose the immoral means. In fact, many consider the failure to do so immoral.

More advanced animals pursue goals and objectives, but man alone pursues ideals. This is a major distinguishing characteristic of the animal, man.

Mechanization versus Automation

Mechanization is the replacement of people's muscle (that is, people as a source of energy) by machines. A machine is a device for applying energy to matter in such a way as to change one or more of its properties. For example, a machine may cut, smooth, cut holes in, reshape or move matter. Changing the characteristics of matter constitutes physical work. Therefore, the Industrial Revolution was about the mechanization of physical work. It is exemplified by the activity that takes place in most factories.

In the nineteenth and twentieth centuries three types of devices were developed which had very significant effects on the activity of people who did not do physical work. First, radar and sonar made observations and generated symbols that represented objects and events. Then there were the telegraph, telephone, wireless, radio and television that transmitted symbols and made communication possible. Finally there was the computer: a way to manipulate symbols logically, that is, in a programmed way. This process of computation is what John Dewey called "thinking". These three functions —observation, communication, and thinking—are functions of mind, not muscle. They do not involve applying energy to matter to change its properties. The application of these devices to the performance of mental tasks is called automation. Automation is fundamentally different in kind than mechanization although many machines are now automated—controlled by devices that perform a mental function. For example, a thermostat controls the operations of furnaces and air conditioners in homes.

The automation of mental tasks is the source of the Post Industrial Revolution. The first Industrial Revolution relieved man of hard physical work; the second relieves man of dull repetitive mental tasks. However, the first and second Industrial Revolutions did not replace the need for people to perform some physical and mental tasks. It relieved them of many that were very difficult, dangerous or otherwise onerous.

The amount of physical work required of populations appears to be decreasing because of mechanization, but the amount of mental "work" appears to be increasing. This requires more and better training and education of the workforce—a requirement that has yet to be completely fulfilled.

The hope was that mechanization and automation would relieve people of many onerous—dull and repetitive—tasks. Those onerous tasks that remain in developed countries are increasingly exported to less developed countries. Unfortunately, the exporting countries have not made a significant effort to replace the jobs lost in this way. They could do so by providing other more productive and demanding tasks. As a result the less well-educated and skilled portions of the populations of more developed countries have suffered either unemployment or downgrading of the work in which they are engaged. There are still many low-skilled jobs that cannot be exported but require doing even in the most advanced countries: for example, garbage collection, janitorial work, caring for gardens and lawns, and road repair. These have become less and less attractive to people whose educational attainment has increased.

The maintenance and upgrading of the infrastructure in more developed countries could well create enough employment to absorb at least as many people as are being lost through outsourcing. Outsourcing remains a vital way of reducing, however slightly, the inequitable distribution of wealth, quality of life, and opportunity among nations. But it has also increased the gap between the advantaged and disadvantaged populations— by increasing maldistribution of wealth, quality of life, and opportunity—within more developed countries.

Messes versus Problems versus Exercises versus Questions

Problems seldom (if ever) exist in isolation. Problems are extracted from reality by analysis. Almost any problem exists as part of a set of interacting problems called by some a mess.

A mess, then, is a system of problems. The characteristics of a mess derive from the interaction of the problems and their solutions, and not from the problems and their solutions taken separately. As is the case with systems, the solution to one part can make the mess worse if its interactions are not taken into account.

A problem is a situation that presents a choice, where what a decision maker does can make a difference in the value of the outcome to him or her, and the decision maker is in doubt as to which choice to make. The problem, then, is which choice yields the best outcome. The hitch is that the solution to a problem that is part of a mess may make the mess worse. On the other hand, the best choice relative to a mess may not require the best solution to any part of it.

Messes, like any system, are best treated as a whole, by design. In design the interactions must be confronted and dealt with, and the objective is dissolution of the mess, not solution of the individual problems of which it consists.

It is difficult for teachers who are trying to teach students how to treat a problem or a mess to arrange for them to work on real ones. Therefore, they generally deal with exercises that are abstracted from problems or messes. An exercise is a formulation of a problem or mess, but where typically all the information required to formulate it is not included. In other words, the choices to which the student is subjected are not realistic.

For example, I was once asked by a prominent statistician to "solve" the following problem. There is a bowl, into which one cannot see, that contains only black and white balls. One reaches in and pulls out m balls of which n are white and, therefore, $m-n$ are black. What is the probability that if I now draw one ball out of the bowl it will be white?

I asked the person who gave me the alleged problem how he knew the bowl contained only black and white balls. He said that was irrelevant to the problem. It wasn't, because if I knew how he knew it contained only black and white balls, I could use that information in answering his question. It was an exercise, not a problem.

So called "case studies" commonly used in teaching law and management are also exercises, not problems or messes. They exclude all the irrelevant information that was filtered out before the problem was formulated. It is precisely the process of filtering out the irrelevant information that is one of the most important parts of problem and mess solving. Therefore, learning how to deal with case studies is like learning how to box with one arm tied behind one's back and then finding oneself in a ring against a boxer who has both hands free!

A question is a still further abstraction, this time from an exercise. The context of the question is withheld from the one who is faced with the question. For example, how much is 3 x 2? If 3 and 2 are logarithms the answer is not 6, but 5.

What color is an object? It depends on the color of the light to which it is exposed. There is never an absolute answer to any question. It always "depends...".

Education suffers if it does not deal with real problems and the messes of which they are a part. This is best done in an apprenticeship with one who has had successful experience in dealing with real problems and messes. Few teachers up to the end of secondary education have had such experience and they do not bring reality into the classroom. One has to go outside of the classroom and school to deal with reality. Surrogates cannot do the job.

A mess can be formulated by assuming no change in the relevant entity's plans, policies and behavior into the future. It also assumes the future that entity expects to come about. Under these conditions every entity will destroy itself. It will do so because under the assumptions it will fail to adapt to a changing (even though expected) environment. Such a demise is known in advance. What is not known in advance is *how* the organization or entity involved will destroy itself. The projection implied by the assumptions will reveal the Achilles heel, the vulnerability of the entity. This is its mess.

For example, the mess formulated for a branch of the Federal Reserve Bank in the 1970s revealed that before the end of the century the bank would require more check clearers than there would be adults in the United States. This clearly could not happen. Some kind of intervention was bound to take place. Should it be the bank or others who intervene? The bank took action and initiated the electronic funds transfer system. This system has reduced the number of checks written to a number that can easily be handled by the bank. It is expected ultimately to eliminate checks.

The mess projected for ALCOA's operations in Tennessee revealed the eventual closing of its operations because of costs arising out of labor-management conflicts. Corporate headquarters was already contemplating closing the operations there. This plus the formulation of the mess led to a profound transformation of labor-management relations. The productivity of the operations increased to a point where the operations became one of the most productive in the world.

The projection of a mess is not a forecast of what will happen, but a forecast either of what cannot happen or of what can be prevented from happening by an intervention. Formulation of its mess provides an organization with a focus for its planning efforts, which should be directed to preventing the demise from occurring. If the organization does not take preventive steps others may take such steps to the detriment of the organization that can, but fails, to act now. Hence the slogan, "Plan or be planned for."

Mission versus Vision

A mission consists of pursuit of a relatively long-range "umbrella" objective that contains all other objectives on the way to attaining it. For example, one corporation has as part of its mission the following: to enable every employee who leaves the company voluntarily, except for retirement, to be more employable than s/he was at the time of initial employment. This commits the company to development of its employees at all levels, to increase their relevant skills and competencies. A South American company formulated the following mission: to demonstrate that a private corporation could contribute significantly to national development. Still another corporation that had operations spread widely over the United States said it wanted to relocate its headquarters and its principal operations to the city in which the company had been formed and from which most of its employees came.

In short, a mission is a cause.

A vision is a picture, verbal or graphic, of what an organization wants to be by a specified time in the future. For example, what kind of activity would the company that wants to contribute to its national development take up eventually? What businesses would it be in? How would it conduct them so as to contribute to national development? In other words, an organization's vision is a concept of what is required organizationally and operationally to accomplish its mission. Visions are in general more detailed than missions.

It is apparent that an organization's mission and vision interact—affect each other—but the mission is normally formulated before the vision. Mission statements are common but most are nothing but platitudes that have no effect on what the organization that states them does. A mission statement that produces no effects in the organization that makes it is a useless and hypocritical appendage.

A mission statement should be unique to the organization that makes it. Most are general statements that apply to many organizations and therefore have no operational value even if they affect the behavior of the organization involved. For example, a statement that an organization wants to be the best without defining what is required to be the best has no operational value. Almost every organization wants to be the best—number one in its field.

A mission statement and a formulated vision are intended to provide direction to an organization. If they do not provide a way of determining whether or not progress, as they define it, is being made, they are useless.

Walking upstairs facing backwards

Need versus Desire

In general, a need is something that is necessary for the attainment of any objective. For example, one may need a pen or pencil and paper to write a letter. One needs a sweater to keep warm. One needs money to buy food.

A need in its more important sense is something necessary for survival, like oxygen, food, and sleep. Many needs in this sense are not desired because people are unaware of them. For example, one needs potassium and iron to survive but many do not know this. Therefore, most people do not desire potassium and iron. Once prescribed by a doctor, however, the need for them becomes conscious, and therefore desired.

To desire something is to want it and pursue it if at all possible. As noted, needs are not necessarily desired. Objects of desire are certainly not all needed.

One cannot want anything without wanting the ability to get it. This ability to get something is called competence. The desire for competence is necessarily a universal desire. No matter what is needed or desired, as long as one desires or needs anything one must want the ability to get it. Recall that this was pointed out in Ethics versus Morality (see page 47). It is reminiscent of the childhood game of answering the question, "If you could satisfy any wish you make, what three wishes would you make?" The clever child usually says s/he needs only one wish: that all his/her wishes would come true.

Objective versus Subjective

Objectivity, contrary to the prevailing opinion, is not obtained by making observations or drawing conclusions that are value free. This is not possible. Objectivity is only obtained when an estimate or conclusion is reached that holds for any and all values brought to bear on it. Objectivity is value-full observation and hypothesis value-full testing. No single observer or scientist can bring all the possible values to bear on his/her observation and thinking. Therefore, objectivity is an ideal pursued by science collectively. It is a property approachable but never to be attained, and approachable only through the interaction of observers and those who test hypotheses with different values.

An observation is subjective when only the interests and properties of the observer are taken into account. It is the absence of objectivity. Most observations have both objective and subjective aspects.

Objectivity-subjectivity is a pair of concepts that can be looked at and discussed separately, but cannot be separated. They have been thought to be separable largely because of a misconception about objectivity. Objectivity has been taken by many to mean an observation made or conclusion drawn from observations without any intervention by the values of the observer. This in effect assumes that the observer, especially a scientist, can check his/her heart outside the laboratory and enter without it. We can neither sense anything nor believe anything without the intervention of our values.

Different observers observe different things when observing what is considered to be the same thing. The differences are attributed to what they bring to their observations, including their values. Therefore, similarity between their observations is attributed to both what they are observing and what they bring to it. This difference has important consequences for two related issues of concern to scientists: conclusions and estimates.

All conclusions extracted from data require a method of estimation. All methods of estimation involve two possible types of error: overestimation and underestimation. Because it is not possible to decrease one without increasing the other, scientists always in effect assume what the relative importance of these two types of error is. This assumption is seldom made consciously. Most scientists are unaware of this assumption and incorrectly assume that it is not made and there is no need for it.

For example, arsenic is used as an ingredient in some pharmaceuticals. Too much can kill. Too little can only make the drug ineffective. Then obviously the two types of error are not equally important. However an estimate of the amount of arsenic in a drug is made, it involves implicitly or explicitly a judgment on the relative importance of the two possible types of error.

Similarly, in testing a hypothesis there are two types of error involved: accepting it when it is false and rejecting it when it is true. Once again, one of these cannot be decreased without increasing the other. Therefore, however a hypothesis is tested, a comparative evaluation, usually implicitly and unconsciously made, of these two types of error is incorporated in drawing a conclusion. What many "testers" do not realize is that there is a balance between these two types of error at which any set of observations can be said to be significant. Significance is not a property of the observations alone but also of the relative importance given to the two types of error, and this is the product of an evaluation.

In ordinary, as well as scientific, judgments it is unconsciously assumed that errors of both types, of equal magnitude, are equally important. This assumption is hardly ever, if ever, true. For example, errors of the same magnitude but of different sign (+ or -) involved in estimating the amount of arsenic in a drug are not equally important. Underestimation of the amount of arsenic in a drug is much more important than an overestimate.

Policy versus Decision

Making a policy is a type of decision but it differs significantly from ordinary decision making. A policy is a rule that governs decision making. Therefore, it commonly takes the form of a law or regulation. For example, the unspoken rule in most companies that no employee can make a higher salary than his/her boss is a policy. Setting an employee's salary is a decision. In a university the rule, hence policy, often is that no one can hold a chair who does not have a PhD. Appointment of someone to a chair is a decision. When a credit card company says that lateness in making payments-due will be penalized, this is a policy. When an individual is charged for lateness, that is a decision.

A decision, of course is a choice from among a set of alternatives (for example, actions, or items on a menu).

At the national level the difference between the responsibilities of the executive and legislative branches of government hangs on the difference between a policy and decision. Congress, the legislative branch, is supposed, in principle, to make policies, not decisions; the executive branch is supposed to make decisions, not policy. The executive branch can suggest policies to Congress and veto policies suggested by Congress, but it cannot make policies. This division is not always clear and adhered to. The executive branch has considerable influence over the policies that are made. On the other hand, Congress has considerable influence over the decisions made by the executive branch.

In general, corporate and institutional boards are also supposed to concentrate on policy, not decisions. But here too this division of labor is often not clear. Nevertheless constitutions and charters are statements of policy, not decisions. The function of boards normally includes managing the organization's interface with its environment. It does so by making policies that are intended to keep the organization in a good relationship with its environment. Congress is expected to make policies that will ensure our nation's relationship with other nations is favorable to them and us. As is apparent, the executive branch can, by its decisions, have a contradictory effect.

Possible versus Probable

Probable is used to designate something that is likely to happen—usually with a better than a fifty-fifty chance. Possible covers anything that has any probability of occurring but is usually restricted to improbable events. Forecasts and predictions try to determine what future is probable. Improbable (less than fifty-fifty) events are covered by assumptions.

One prepares for what are considered to be probable events with specific plans. The number of probable futures is often small enough to permit such planning for each of them to take place. Not so for possible events. There are usually too many to plan for each of these. Rather, the development of a rapid response capability is the way these are usually treated.

For example, in driving between cities our getting there depends on what a large number of other drivers do. Any one of them could obstruct our trip. But we don't forecast what each will do. Rather we learn how to respond to whatever they do that affects us rapidly and effectively. On the other hand, we would prepare uniquely for likely events such as rain, by carrying an umbrella, or snow, by salting the roads.

PRACTICE VERSUS CASE STUDIES

Most educators agree that the best way to learn a professional practice is to practice it, through on-the-job learning. But since most educators believe they cannot provide such an opportunity to most, if not all, of their students, they settle for use of case studies. A case study is a detailed description of a real problem that the students can discuss. Through discussion they reach a conclusion about what they would do in the situation described. They are allegedly guided in this exercise by the "teacher" who knows what actually was done and what happened as a result. This is generally revealed at the end of the exercise.

Most of those who were actually involved in the problem described in the case are flabbergasted when they read the case. They are surprised at how much is left out and how important what is left out was. Separating the relevant from the irrelevant inputs in problem-solving is one of its most difficult and important aspects. In this sense the case study is a very important distortion of reality. But it is not the only one.

When managers are shown a write-up of a case in which they were involved they often find that it leaves out the difficulty in *implementing* any solution that is proposed. They characterize the case as a problem set in a vacuum rather than a real organizational space. The problem they say is not to learn how to find a solution to a problem but how to find a solution to a problem that can be implemented.

Case studies are very poor surrogates for reality. (See Messes versus Problems versus Exercises versus Questions, pages 82-86.) They give students a false sense of security when they approach a real problem in a real situation. Then they have to revise what they have learned. This is not only difficult, but it can be demoralizing. They have been misled.

Professional versus Nonprofessional Employees

A profession is identified by (1) its possession of a body of specified knowledge that is not generally shared by those outside the profession, and (2) a set of standards applicable to where and how they practice and whom they affect. Therefore, a professional who is employed by another person or organization will not violate the standards for the sake of his/her employer.

For example, a physician employed by a corporation may discover asbestos (a serious threat to health) in one of the company's major facilities. The company would not like to have this reported because its repair would be very costly. In addition, there are likely to be suits brought against the company that could also be costly. A professional physician would rather be fired or resign than let the condition go unreported.

An employee who is not a professional or a professional who acts unprofessionally might keep the discovery quiet. The interests of the employer are placed above those of the profession and those they are supposed to serve.

Many professionals refuse to be employed by others when they think such problems cannot be avoided. The perceived morality of a profession is based on judgments about the extent to which their standards are placed above those of employers or clients. For this reason, lawyers are often believed to be less moral than physicians, and physicians more moral than corporate executives. In fact, managers, and particularly executives, are not generally considered to be professionals, although they usually consider themselves to be.

Pure versus Applied Science

This is a distinction that has been very hard to make precise. To assert that pure science is science the results of which have no application, is not adequate because many results that appear inapplicable at the time they are produced become applicable later. For example, Georg Cantor thought, and was proud of the fact, that his work on transfinite numbers had no applicability. Einstein later found an application for them.

The results of pure science are generally intended for use only by other scientists. Once an application is found for a finding of allegedly pure science, it is no longer considered to be pure. From this it follows that the distinction is not inherent in the nature of the research but in the way its output is used. This may change over time.

Scientists who engage in what they think is pure research tend to think the kind of research they do is more difficult than that performed by applied scientists. This gave those engaged in allegedly pure research a feeling of superiority over applied scientists. However, it has increasingly become apparent that the use of difficulty to define or characterize pure science has no validity. Furthermore, the distinction, whatever it is based on, has become increasingly difficult to maintain. For example, is research on global warming pure or applied? Is it more or less difficult than other types of research?

Developmental research is research that attempts to find applications, or an application, of findings of alleged pure science. Many inventions are based on research of this type. Perhaps the work of Edison exemplifies this. We tend to call such developmental research "technology". Technology delivers to us the values of scientific research—pure or impure.

Rational versus Irrational

Irrationality is a quality of thinking often attributed to those who do not agree with us. We seldom attribute this difference to a difference in the objectives, but we should. For example, representatives of the Ford Foundation found the (Asian) Indian practice of having large families (average 6+) irrational because it kept per capita wealth from growing. The large number of children born each year diluted national increases in wealth, which were considerable. On the other hand, Indians found that at least two employed sons were required to support two unemployed parents. Because of infant mortality and the fact that half those born were female—and eventually unemployable—the average size of a family required was six. Adult males became unemployable quite early because of the oversupply of young workers to replace older ones, and the lack of any form of social security other than that provided by one's family.

The correctness of this explanation was proved by the fact that Indian families that had three sons in a row generally had no more children. Those that had three females in a row were just getting started. The problem was not birth control but the lack of social security.

What is irrational from one point of view may be quite rational from another. Therefore, wherever there is an apparent difference between two parties on rationality it is worth examining their objectives. Rationality and irrationality are not properties of judgments but of the points of view dictated by a difference in objectives of those making the judgments.

In the United States there is a considerable divide in the public between those who condone torture of terrorists during their interrogation and those who don't. Each considers the other to be irrational. These judgments follow from the relative seriousness with which they consider security and human rights. Different values produce different judgments. It is fruitless to argue about the judgments. The values behind them are the issue. These are very difficult to change. But realizing their role in the different judgments makes discussion more reasonable.

Reactive versus Inactive versus Proactive versus Interactive

These terms are best understood in the context of planning or problem solving. In reactive (reactionary) planning a previous state or condition is targeted for revival. A plan to realize that state or condition creates a path that goes from where one is now back to where one once was. Reactive problem solving tries to resolve problems. It is based on past experience in one of two ways. In the first, a previous problem similar to the one that is current is recalled. Then the previous way of treating the problem is identified. A determination is then made as to whether that treatment should be used "as is" or requires modification in light of situational differences or what has been learned in the interim.

Alternatively a determination is made of who or what is to blame for the problem. Then, if the cause or producer of the problem can be identified and removed, the problem solver is back where s/he was before the problem was created. In both cases the solution sought is not necessarily the best, but is one thought to be "good enough". Such a solution is said to "satisfice", to satisfy and suffice. The methods used by reactive planners and problem solvers are normally qualitative, judgmental and based on common sense.

Proactive (liberal) planners produce one or more forecasts of the future and then, given these, develop a vision of where they want to be in (usually) five or ten years. Then they plan a set of actions intended to transform the "now" into the desired "then". In proactive problem solving an effort is made to do better than good enough: to do as well as possible, to optimize.

The methods used by proactive problem solvers tend to be scientific, including experimentation and the use of mathematical modeling. Therefore, they tend to go beyond common sense and qualitative judgment.

An inactive (conservative) planner or problem solver wants to keep things much as they are. Therefore, they try to prevent change and the need for it. When conditions require that something be done, they try to do as little as possible. In effect, the conservative planner is an anti-planner and avoids dealing with problems as much as possible. S/he often does nothing and hopes problems will solve themselves or go away on their own initiative.

Recently a fourth type of planning has been developed—interactive. The interactive (radical) planner and problem solver first produces a vision of where s/he would be right now if s/he were free to be wherever s/he wanted with virtually no constraints. Then s/he plans to approximate this vision as closely as possible by what s/he does now. S/he goes into the future constantly trying to close the gap between where s/he is and where s/he would like to be ideally now.

The interactive type tries to dissolve problems by redesigning the entity that has them or its environment in such a way as to eliminate the problem and the possibility of its reoccurring. (See ABSOLUTION VERSUS RESOLUTION VERSUS SOLUTION VERSUS DISSOLUTION, pages 1-3.)

Reflex versus Reaction versus Response

A reflex is an act that is caused–determined—by its stimulus. It does not involve choice or even require consciousness. The rapid withdrawal of a hand accidentally placed on a hot stove is a reflex. Ducking to avoid the ball from hitting one in the face, or trying to catch one that is thrown lower, is also a reflex.

A response is behavior produced by something preceding it. The producer was necessary but not sufficient for the behavior that follows. Choice is necessarily involved; there are alternative ways of responding. For example, we can respond either favorably or unfavorably to a newspaper article, a book or a television program.

A reaction is a habitual response. Habits, of course, can be broken. Therefore, reactions occur in situations in which a choice is possible but is not made. There is no deliberation. For example, a person may always carry an umbrella when it is raining out of doors. Choice of an umbrella is not necessary; one can choose an alternative when an umbrella is not available.

Reflexes, responses, and reactions are different types of behavior. If we want to change a person's behavior it is very important to know what type of behavior we are trying to change. It is virtually impossible to change a reflex. To change a reaction, one must break a habit. This too can be very difficult. It requires raising habitual behavior (which is usually unconscious) to consciousness. Responses are the easiest to change, but not necessarily easy.

Changing them requires convincing the responder that a better response—one that is more efficient or with a better outcome—is available.

In military training a great deal of effort goes into converting responses that involve choice into reactions, in fact, into almost reflexes. Obedience becomes an end-in-itself. In education, however, the objective should be to enlarge the sets of alternatives from which a person can and does make choices in any situation.

Reform versus Transform

To reform a system is to change its behavior without changing its structure or its functions. It continues to do the kinds of things it has always done but does some of them differently. To transform a system is to change its structure and the way it functions. The changes it produces are radical (go to the roots of the system) or even revolutionary.

Reformations and transformations are both intended to improve performance of that which has been modified.

Transformations of any type of social group require leadership because they involve a risk. Therefore, they also require a willingness on the part of followers to make short-run sacrifices in order to make longer-term gains. The willingness to make such sacrifices requires a vision supplied by the leader of the end-point of the transformation. It must be an inspiring vision and one that is accompanied by a formulation of a strategy for making progress toward its realization.

A reformation does not require a leader; managers can usually make it happen. Inspiration is seldom required. A tactical plan is usually sufficient to bring it about; a strategy is not necessary. A manager who can exercise authority can frequently bring a reformation about with subordinates who do not necessarily follow voluntarily (as is required in a transformation). Transformations may be led by leaders who have absolutely no authority over their followers. If the leader of a transformation exercises authority it is authority voluntarily given to him/her by his/her followers.

The change of an autocratic monarchy or dictatorship to a democracy is a transformation. The change of a democracy from conservative to liberal is a reformation. The change of Christianity from Catholicism to Protestantism was also a transformation but was called a Reformation. The change from Methodism to Baptism was a reformation. The Industrial Revolution transformed societies. Changes in a nation's constitution, in contrast to additions, usually transform the nation. Additions to a constitution may or may not do so. Perestroika and glasnost were transforming in the Soviet Union but they have been diluted (reformed) since.

Science versus Humanities

Science and the humanities are two sides of the same coin: they can be viewed and discussed separately but they cannot be separated.

Science is the search for similarities among things that are apparently different. The humanities search for differences among things that are apparently similar.

The scientific law of gravity, for example, describes how any body regardless of size, shape, or material will fall in a vacuum. Differences among the bodies are irrelevant in a vacuum. In the real world, which is not a vacuum, a feather and an iron ball will fall at different speeds. Here the difference between a feather and an iron ball is very important in understanding how they fall in a normal environment.

In branches of the humanities—for example, autobiography, art, and history—an effort is made to differentiate between individuals and events. Literature generally deals with unique people and events. History makes apparent the differences between eras and ages, and between times and places where events take place. The humanities (including art) dwell on uniqueness.

Understanding an individual person, object or event requires that we understand both how it is unique and what it has in common with other persons, objects, and events. In studying a particular person, for example, we begin by finding what properties s/he has. These properties place him or her in classes of individuals with similar properties. Every introvert is unique but is also a member of a class of personality types. We can apply what is known about introversion generally to the individual but to be effective we must also take into account the uniqueness of the individual.

The interplay of science and the humanities is particularly apparent in practices that treat—design, build, maintain or repair—individual objects and events. For example, a good engineer must be aware of the unique characteristics of the site of a new bridge as well as the structural laws that allow him to design a bridge for that site. S/he must consider the aesthetics of his/her design as well as its structure. Similarly, a physician must know the nature of a person's ailments or disability, but to treat them effectively s/he must take such unique characteristics of the patient into account as allergies, underweight-overweight, age, and previous ailments.

Science pursues its objective by conducting inquiries. However, inquiries can be carried out using common sense. The difference between common sense and scientific inquiry is control.

To the extent to which inquiry is controlled (efficient) it is scientific. Therefore, the difference between science and common-sense inquiry is a matter of degree. Common-sense inquiry and scientific inquiry do not form a dichotomy but are positions on a scale of control.

Selling versus Marketing

To sell a product or service is to exchange it for money with a purchaser: the customer. Sales involves inducing, negotiating or facilitating a purchase of a product or service. Sales may involve bidding for a contract.

Marketing involves all the steps required to make a sale of a product or service possible. Depending on the nature of the product or service involved it may include pricing, distribution, advertising, promotion, displays at the point of sale, and maintaining it once it is in use.

The producer of a product or service may sell it directly to the ultimate user, or go through a wholesaler and/or a retailer in order to reach an ultimate customer. All the intermediate stages of getting a product or service to its user may be owned by the producer or by independent businesses.

Signs versus Symbols versus Signals

A sign is something that produces a response to something other than itself. That to which the sign produces a response is the signification of a sign. The denotation of a sign is the set of objects or events signified by a sign. The connotation of a sign is the set of properties of the things denoted by a sign to which it produces a response.

The denotation of "the current president of the United States" is the person Barrack Obama. The connotation of these words depends on one's political evaluation of the president's performance: good, bad or indifferent. Words like "my father" have different denotations to unrelated people but may have the same connotations.

A symbol is a sign that produces a response to something that is in turn a producer of a response to something other than itself. For example, "+" is a symbol of the sign "plus". Similarly, ">" is a sign of "is greater than". Therefore, a symbol may be a sign of a sign. For example, the cross is a familiar symbol of the word "Christ". The response to the symbol is a response to the sign "Christ".

A signal is a symbol that produces an intended response. It is an instruction. A red light is a directive to stop and a green is a directive to go. Signals tell us where we can and can't go, what we can and can't do. The siren on an ambulance or fire truck tells us to get out of the way.

The meaning of a sign is the set of functional properties of the response it produces. That is, its meaning lies in the functional difference it makes in its respondent's behavior. When someone cries "Fire" in a theater, its meaning does not lie in the flames that the cry signifies but in their significance: it makes people try to get out of the theater. A sign may have different meanings to different individuals and different meanings to the same individual at different times. Telling the people in a theater, for example, that it is on fire has a different meaning to them than telling it to the fire department. While those in the theater try to get out, the firemen try to get in.

Strategy versus Tactics

Strategy and tactics have to do with the kinds of choices an individual or group makes. The difference between them is multidimensional.

First, the more of an organization that is affected by a decision, the more strategic that decision is. Any decision made in a division or department of an organization is less strategic than one made at the top. That which may be taken as a strategic decision in a department may be considered to be tactical at a higher level of the organization.

Second, the longer the effects of the decision will last the more strategic it is. Short-run operating decisions tend to be tactical.

Decisions that will have effects that extend beyond a year tend to be strategic.

Third, the greater the magnitude of the effect of a decision the more strategic it is. At the extreme, an organization's life-and-death decisions are strategic. Taking care of a machine that is not working properly is tactical. Finally, strategic decisions tend to deal with effectiveness: the value of outcomes. Tactical decisions tend to deal with efficiency: the likelihood of producing an outcome. Using concepts previously introduced, tactical decisions are concerned with doing things right. Strategic decisions are concerned with doing the right things.

It is apparent, therefore, that strategy and tactics form no simple dichotomy. These are relative concepts depending very much on where the decision maker sits.

System versus Network

A system is a whole that is defined by its function in a larger system of which it is a part.

> (An automobile, for example, is defined for its role in the transportation system; a university by its role in the educational system.)

It has at least two essential parts—parts without which it could not perform its defining function.

> For example, an automobile cannot function without a motor, fuel, pump or battery. A person cannot function without a brain, lungs, and a heart.

The essential parts have five essential characteristics:

1. Each can affect the behavior or properties of the whole.

2. The way an essential part affects the whole depends on what at least one other part is doing. The effects of the parts are interdependent.

3. Every two essential parts are connected, directly or indirectly.

4. Subsets of essential parts (subsystems) also can affect the properties or behavior of the whole and the way they affect the whole depends on at least one other subsystem.

5.   There is a direct or indirect connection between every pair of subsystems.

It follows that a system is a whole that cannot be divided into independent parts. Its properties and behavior derive from the interactions of its parts, not their actions considered separately.

A network is a whole whose function is to enable communication between its parts. In a well-designed network there is a connection between every possible pair of parts. But in a network, unlike a system, there are no essential parts. If any part is removed there are alternative ways to connect the parts affected.

The parts of a system may form a network but not every network is a system. The so-called "telephone system" is not a system but a network. It has no essential parts. However, a telephone company is a system.

If a collection of parts is neither a system nor a network it is an aggregation, like a crowd or inventory of parts.

For example, consider the wired telephone network. If the connection between Philadelphia and New York is broken, one can still reach New York from Philadelphia by going through any number of other cities: for example, Trenton, New Brunswick, and Newark.

But if an essential part of a system—for example, the motor from an automobile—is broken the automobile cannot perform its function.

Teaching versus Learning

Education is an admirable thing, but it is well to remember from time to time that nothing that is worth knowing can be taught.

Oscar Wilde, *The Critic as Artist*

Being taught is one of the worst ways to learn anything. The Association of Research Libraries in Washingon, D.C. supported this assertion with the following "numbers" published in 1996. People in a learning situation retain:

- 10% of what they read
- 20% of what they hear
- 30% of what they see and hear
- 70% of what they talk over with others
- 80% of what they use and do in real life
- 90% of what they teach someone else to do

These "numbers" make it clear that being taught is not a very effective way of learning, but that teaching others is very efficient. In the one-room schoolhouses of the past, students taught students. No one teacher could manage the material for students at every age level.

The overwhelming majority of schools are upside down because they assume one learns what is being taught. If anything, some of what is taught is memorized and retained for only a very short time. To remember is not the same as learning. Something is learned if it can be used effectively to attain a desired end. Despite this, very little of formal education involves this type of learning. There are exceptions: medical and veterinary internships and the years of architectural practice before licensing can be acquired. At one time professionals were educated exclusively in apprenticeships. Most of the great artists honed their skills in apprenticeships, not in schools.

> *The pupil is... "schooled" to confuse teaching with learning, grade advancement with education, a diploma with competence, and fluency with the ability to say something new.*
>
> **Ivan Illich, *Deschooling Society***

Training is education by doing. It is restricted to imparting a skill, a capability such as playing a sport, woodworking, cooking, and so on. Of course one cannot learn history this way but one can learn languages this way. There is no better way to learn a language than immersion in a society in which the language to be learned is used almost exclusively.

On-the-job training is a particularly effective way of learning. It is widely recognized that most, if not nearly all, of what people use in their jobs they learned on their jobs.

Business schools do not teach students how to manage. What they do teach are (1) vocabularies that enable students to speak with authority about subjects they do not understand, and (2) to use principles of management that have demonstrated their ability to withstand any amount of disconfirming evidence. The only justification of these schools is the tickets of admission they provide to jobs where something about management can be learned. The same can be said about schools of architecture and city planning. Three great American architects—Richardson, Sullivan, and Frank Lloyd Wright—did not learn architecture in schools, but in practice. Most great statisticians learned statistics when their work in other fields required that they use statistics that did not exist. R. A. Fisher is a case in point; he developed designed experiments in an agricultural context. These designs enabled experimenters to take into account the effects of a collection of relevant variables that are not dealt with separately in the experiment. This development opened up the possibility of experimentation in area in which it had previously not been possible.

Tools versus Techniques versus Methods of Inquiry

The tools of scientific or common sense inquiry are the physical and conceptual instruments that are used in conducting it. Computers, microscopes, tables of random numbers, tape measures, scales, thermometers, and MRI machines are among the physical tools used in inquiry. Mathematics and logic are among the conceptual tools used in inquiry. In general, bodies of knowledge and understanding, such as exist in a variety of disciplines, are among the most important tools of inquiry.

A technique of inquiry is a course of action that employs a tool as a means to the end sought by the inquiry. In other words, the techniques of inquiry are ways of using the tools of inquiry. They are the behavior of the inquirer. Random sampling, differentiation, measurement, land and market surveying, graphic analysis, and doing an MRI or EKG are among the techniques used in the practice of inquiry.

Methods of inquiry are ways of selecting the techniques to use in conducting an inquiry. The methodology of inquiry is the logic employed in selecting the way inquiry is conducted. For example, methods include ways of selecting an experimental or sampling design, and a way of measuring hardness, intelligence or cooperation, and a way of selecting the medical tests to employ in pursuit of a diagnosis.

The methodology of science also goes under the name "philosophy of science". Among other things, it deals with the assumptions about the nature of reality and inquiry that affect the choices made in conducting inquiry. For example, it considers such things as whether one should employ analysis or synthesis, and proceed inductively or deductively. The branch of philosophy called epistemology is also concerned with ways of acquiring knowledge and understanding.

The more an inquirer knows about tools, techniques, and methods of inquiry, the more control s/he can exercise in conducting inquiry.

About the Author

Russell Lincoln Ackoff (12 February 1919 – 29 October 2009) was one of the 20th century's foremost organizational theorists, a respected consultant and Anheuser-Busch Professor Emeritus of Management Science at The Wharton School, University of Pennsylvania. Ackoff was a pioneer in the field of Operations Research, Systems Thinking and Management Science.

He completed his undergraduate studies in Architecture at the University of Pennsylvania in 1941. From 1942 to 1946 he served in the US Army, stationed in the Philippines. He returned to study at the University of Pennsylvania, where he received his doctorate in philosophy of science in 1947 as C. West Churchman's first doctoral student, and also taught logic. From 1967 onwards, he received a number of honorary doctorates.

His career in Operations Research began at the end of the 1940s. His 1957 book *Introduction to Operations Research*, co-authored with C. West Churchman and Leonard Arnoff, helped to define the field. Ackoff was president of the Operations Research Society of America in 1956–1957 and president of the International Society for the Systems Sciences in 1987.

His seminal work on Systems and Design Thinking, *Creating the Corporate Future,* was published in 1981. Throughout his career, he wrote numerous books on Systems Management, including *Ackoff's Best, Re-Creating the Corporation, Turning Learning Right Side Up*, co-authored with Daniel Greenberg, and *Management f-Laws*, co-authored with Herbert J. Addison and Sally Bibb.

A founding member of the Institute of Management Sciences, his work in consulting and education involved more than 350 corporations and 75 government agencies in the United States and beyond. Management grandee, he was voted one of the world's most influential business thinkers in a recent poll by the *Harvard Business Review*.

BY THE SAME AUTHOR:

Management f-Laws ~ Russell Ackoff (with Herbert Addison and Sally Bibb)

In the same vein as Sod's Law and Parkinson's Law, here are 80 of Russ Ackoff's subversive insights into the world of business and organizations, with ripostes from Sally Bibb.

Systems Thinking for Curious Managers ~ Russell Ackoff (with Herbert Addison and Andrew Carey)

An introduction to Systems Thinking and Russ Ackoff's view of organizations, including 40 more, previously unpublished, management f-laws.

Memories ~ Russell Ackoff

A collection of stories, drawn from Ackoff's own life experience, each of which is used to illustrate a belief, principle or conclusion central to his theories of Systems Thinking and Design Thinking.

ON SYSTEMS AND DESIGN THINKING:

The Innovation Acid Test: Growth Through Design and Differentiation ~ Andrew Jones

How Design Thinking underpins the world's most dynamic, successful companies, and how to apply it any organization.

Systems Thinking in the Public Sector ~ John Seddon

A devastating critique of targets, incentives, inspection, economies of scale, shared back-office services and "deliverology" in public services.

The Search for Leadership: An Organisational Perspective ~ William Tate

Explains why conventional leadership models miss the point and presents a Systems Thinking approach that focuses on the organization rather than individual leaders.

Delivering Public Services that Work ~ Peter Middleton with John Seddon

A ground-breaking collection of Case Studies showing how Systems Thinking has been applied to a particular public service in six local authorities.

Economies of Life: Patterns of Health and Wealth ~ Bill Sharpe

Argues that there are many economies, (not just the one based on money), and that they all contribute to the health and sustainability of our shared lives. In this model, money is the currency of trade and art is the currency of experience.

About Triarchy Press

Triarchy Press is an independent publishing house that looks at how organizations work and how to make them work better. We present challenging perspectives on organizations in short and pithy, but rigorously argued, books.

Through our books, pamphlets and website we aim to stimulate ideas by encouraging real debate about organizations in partnership with people who work in them, research them or just like to think about them.

Please tell us what you think about the ideas in this book at:

www.triarchypress.com/telluswhatyouthink

If you feel inspired to write – or have already written – an article, a pamphlet or a book on any aspect of organizational theory or practice, we'd like to hear from you. Submit a proposal at:

www.triarchypress.com/writeforus

For more information about Triarchy Press, or to order any of our publications, please visit our website or drop us a line:

www.triarchypress.com

We're on Twitter:

@TriarchyPress

and Facebook:

www.facebook.com/triarchypress

tp